BEYOND THE SPOTLIGHT

On the Road With Phyllis Diller

Robin Skone-Palmer

Wigeon Publishing
San Diego

Copyright © 2013 by Robin Skone-Palmer

All rights reserved. No part of this book may be reproduced or transmitted in any form or by any means, electronic or mechanical, including photocopying, recording, or by any information storage and retrieval system, without permission in writing from the publisher.

Wigeon Publishing
San Diego, California
www.WigeonPublishing.com

First Edition: April 1, 2013

ISBN-10: 0985972882

ISBN-13: 978-0-9859728-8-2

Library of Congress Control Number: 2013934392

Cover by Tim Brittain

Cover photo courtesty of the Phyllis Diller estate.
All rights reserved.

Back cover photos courtesy of Ingrid Chapman.
All rights reserved.

Printed in the United States of America

To my brother, John
(Skonie to the rest of the world)
who never lost faith in me.
He read the original manuscript many
years ago and would be thrilled to see it
now as a real, live, published book.

Thanks, big brother.

Author's Note

Phyllis Diller was unlike anybody I'd met before—not because she was a celebrity, but because of her determination, her drive, her absolute faith in herself, and her firm belief that she could be and do anything she set her mind to. She was like a force of nature—unstoppable and at times overwhelming.

Phyllis was never a quitter. Even after she retired from the stage, she continued to work, turning her talent to painting. She sold her paintings at auctions and to collectors and donated many to charitable events. The last time I was in her house, just a year before she died, she invited me to view her studio, which was filled with canvases both large and small. She had set up the room with easels that held an assortment of works-in-progress, and tables that were covered with brushes and paints. Phyllis had stacked canvases, some finished, some not, against the walls. One large painting that she called *Buttons* stood on the easel by the door. Her paintings lined the upstairs hallway leading to what had once been my office.

After Phyllis died, I read the comments attached to the obituaries in both the *New York Times* and the *Los Angeles Times*. I was struck by how many people had sweet memories of Phyllis and stories to share and the love for her that poured forth. Phyllis was indeed an American icon. I started to add my own comments but soon realized I would need a book to record my thoughts. Then I reminded myself that I had already done that.

During the time I worked for Phyllis, she often said, "Robin, you should write a book." Several years later, I did. I sent it to her. She read it and wrote an endorsement, but as anyone who has ever tried to get a book published knows, it is difficult. For many years, this manuscript has languished in the bottom drawer of my dresser under a pile of socks.

When I worked for Phyllis, people often asked me, "What's Phyllis Diller really like?" Now that Phyllis has left us, I wanted to share the "real Phyllis Diller" with her fans and admirers. I hope you enjoy reading about her life off-stage and are as impressed with this remarkable woman as are those of us who worked with her. She truly was one of a kind.

1

A high wall surrounded the mansion on South Rockingham Avenue in Brentwood. A small plaque by the curb displayed the house number. I checked the address I'd scrawled on a piece of scratch paper.

Yes, this is the place.

The gate stood open and I pulled my secondhand Volkswagen onto the beautifully patterned brick forecourt and parked a safe distance from a sleek gray Jaguar. I looked at my watch and saw that in spite of getting lost on the meandering streets of Brentwood, I was pretty close to on time.

I clutched my résumé in one hand and checked my makeup in the rearview mirror. As I walked down the path toward the front door, I glimpsed a sporty convertible and a Rolls Royce under a carport off to the side.

Strange that the house didn't face the street—rather, it looked south toward a large green lawn surrounded by manicured bushes and very tall trees. To the west I could see only trees but knew I was atop a bluff a couple of miles from the Pacific Ocean. Perhaps if the trees weren't there, I could actually see the water. I took a few deep breaths and inhaled the tangy salt air. A nice change from smoggy Los

Angeles. I tried to be calm, not to think about the fact that I could be walking into a life-changing experience.

For the past few months I'd been working at a series of temporary jobs. Prior to that, I had spent five years as a secretary for the U.S. Department of State in the Foreign Service, first at the American Embassy in Pretoria, South Africa, then at the Embassy in London.

Ah, yes, London in the swingin' '60s.

I'd spent a total of five years overseas and at the age of twenty-eight decided I didn't want to live in foreign countries all my life. In the Foreign Service, popular wisdom says that if you stay for more than two tours, you will never be able to leave. Living abroad on an American salary is living royally. I knew I would have a hard time giving up all of those advantages—the maids, the travel, the money to buy designer clothes, and so much more, but I loved America and Americans. I was colossally homesick, and in 1970 I bid the Foreign Service good-bye and came back to live with my parents in North Hollywood, California. This had not been an easy decision, and one of my great fears was that I would never have a job as exciting as the one I had just left. The idea of being stuck in some dead-end job in, say, an insurance company, gave me the heebie-jeebies. The irony was that at the time I was filling in for the executive secretary to the vice president of a large insurance company.

Thank heaven the man I worked for could tell I didn't fit in. "You need to get a really good job," he said one day. I agreed, but what? "I'd like to put you in touch with the employment agency we use. They're very good, and I'm sure they can find you something you like."

I hoped he was right.

The lady at the employment agency was nice, thorough, and said she'd call me when something turned up. She called the next morning.

"Do you still have your passport?" she asked.

"Yes," I assured her, although it wasn't the whole truth, but I didn't think I needed to bother this nice lady with silly details.

"I have a job with someone who travels a lot. She's leaving for London next week and her secretary just quit. I think you'd be perfect."

I nearly dropped the phone. I swear my heart skipped a beat.

"Can you go this afternoon for an interview?"

"Yes! Yes! Absolutely. Of course!"

"It's close to where you are now, in Brentwood." She gave me directions to the house. "When you get there, ask for Phyllis Diller."

2

I stood between tall white pillars on a small front porch edged with bowls of colorful flowers. I could hear door chimes echoing inside. A petite lady with blond hair opened the door. She looked decidedly nervous. Could this be Phyllis Diller? I'd not had a television for the past five years, so I wasn't quite sure what a Phyllis Diller was, but I had heard the name. Some kind of celebrity, for sure.

The lady introduced herself—Val, the housekeeper. Val assured me that Miss Diller would be along shortly. She was at lunch with Marc London, the head writer of *Laugh-In*, and seemed to be running a little late. Val showed me to a seat in the living room, which was filled with dozens of red roses. It featured a grand piano at one end and an almost life-size painting of Bob Hope at the other. Val offered me a drink, which I declined, then she excused herself, once again telling me that Miss Diller would be along shortly.

From where I sat I could see that the house was built around a formal courtyard with a fountain and wrought-iron love seat. I considered that there could hardly be a less ideal place for a courtship because nearly every room of the house seemed to look out onto the courtyard.

The appointment was for one o'clock, and by two o'clock I concluded Miss Diller would be more than a little late. Val popped in from time to time, offering refreshment and reassurances. The later it became, the more nervous Val became. The more nervous Val became, the calmer I became. By four o'clock, when Miss Diller returned home, I was starting to get slightly bored. Val was a wreck.

Miss Diller entered the room in a swirl of multicolored silk, smiled, and apologized for being late. She took my résumé, scanned it quickly, and right away told me she was impressed by my Foreign Service background, intrigued by my hyphenated name, and pleased to note that I was an experienced traveler. Although my initial apprehension had returned when I'd heard the front door open, I relaxed almost immediately. She seemed very nice and was as normal as any employer interviewing a prospective secretary.

"There's a lot of traveling in this job," she warned me. I tried to look serious, as if somehow this might be bad. "My last secretary couldn't take the pressure," she continued. "She left me stranded in New Orleans."

(I found out later that Phyllis had indulged in hyperbole; she never traveled alone. In addition to the secretary, she usually had her husband, her wardrobe mistress, and occasionally one of her teenage children.)

We'd talked for about ten minutes when Phyllis's husband, Warde, came in. He had been putting away his car—an Excalibur Roadster, an expensive sports car that looked like a 1929 Mercedes-Benz. A wedding present from Phyllis, I later found out.

He should have been handsome; he was tall and slim with stunning blue eyes in a well-shaped face, but it was distorted by a sneer. He looked rather outlandish, dressed in a stretch lace shirt, tight pants, and tightly curled gray hair. He radiated condescension, which I found surprising for someone who wore stretch lace shirts. He took my résumé from Phyllis and skimmed over it.

"Well," he announced, "this looks very good, but you must realize that Madam (it turned out he always called her that in front of the help) has many people to interview. We'll have to let you know."

That startled me. I thought Phyllis and I were getting along quite well.

Phyllis also appeared taken aback. "Warde, please let me finish talking to this young lady."

"Ada," he said, "I need to talk to you."

Who is Ada, I wondered.

Phyllis went out into the hall with her husband and I overheard a ferocious battle being carried on in whispers. It wasn't long before Warde returned to the living room to dismiss me. Phyllis was not with him.

"You must understand," he told me, "Madam can't just hire the first person who applies. This is a very specialized position. You can check with the agency and they'll let you know." He left the room and Val appeared to show me out. As she walked with me to the front door, I could hear Warde's raised voice. Phrases like "you have to listen to me" and "you don't know what you're doing" floated down the hallway. I didn't know if I wanted this job or not.

The lady at the employment agency called me the next day. "You've been offered the job with Miss Diller."

I hesitated a moment as I remembered the sneer on Warde's face and his high-handed manner, then I looked around the little windowless cubicle where I was sitting. I thought about my brand-new passport and traveling, doing something really different.

"Okay," I said with perhaps less enthusiasm than she expected.

"I don't have all the details," she went on. "I'll give you the phone number of Miss Diller's attorney in New York."

I asked my current boss if I could place a long-distance call, and he not only agreed, but said I could use his office for privacy.

When I reached the attorney, Mr. B, he named a pretty low salary. I thought a celebrity would pay more, but Mr. B explained that Miss Diller felt there were plenty of perks that came from working for her—the travel, the excitement, and the opportunity to do things that were out of the ordinary. Also, he added, there was a ten-dollar per diem for every day we traveled. That was to cover the cost of meals and other necessities, such as dry cleaning, when we were in hotels.

I guessed it was okay. I knew I didn't want to keep working in a nine-to-five job, and working for Phyllis Diller seemed fun and adventurous. It would be different from anything I'd done before and different was good.

I asked Mr. B if there was insurance or other benefits. He snorted—or perhaps it was a laugh. Apparently, the glamour of working for Miss Diller was supposed to trump all other considerations. Still, it definitely appealed to me and seemed too good to pass up. I'd wanted something out of the ordinary and this certainly was that. I agreed to the salary and Mr. B told me to be at the house at 9:00 A.M. Monday.

3

Monday morning I arrived full of anticipation and some trepidation.

"Phyllis and Warde left for London on Saturday," Val told me as she ushered me in. "They took Karen with them. She's Phyllis's wardrobe mistress."

I'd been looking forward to going back to London and had rushed through my passport renewal. (When I left the Department of State job, my Official Passport had been canceled, and I had to get a new one.) I swallowed my disappointment and told myself it was probably just as well that I'd have time to settle in before they got back. I later learned that Karen loathed London as much as I loved it.

Val took me upstairs to the back of the house to a little room with a slanted ceiling. "This is your office," Val said and gestured toward an older woman seated at a desk. "This is Maria. She's the home secretary."

Maria stood and shook my hand. "It's nice to meet you," she said in a softly accented voice.

The room was tiny and I guessed it had been designed as a nursery. Two desks and four filing cabinets filled the entire space. Our desks were arranged back-to-back so we faced each other.

Over the next few days I learned Maria's story, which was somewhat gothic. She came from a wealthy family who had a grand home in Mexico City. She had been raised a "lady," so had no skills or trade, and after a disastrous reversal of fortune and a short, unhappy marriage, found herself on her own. She and her sister moved to the States, where they learned to type and got jobs as secretaries and occasionally translators. Maria ended up as the "home secretary" to Phyllis Diller. I felt that in true gothic-novel tradition, there should be a handsome son to rescue her, but although Phyllis's son was quite handsome, he was still in his teens.

Val then took me downstairs to the kitchen, which was painted bright red and had red appliances. It sort of startled me.

"This is where we take our breaks," she said, motioning to a small dinette. "You get here at nine and work till five, with an hour for lunch. We take breaks in the morning and afternoon." Val went on to introduce me to Tina and Mary, the maids who worked under Val. Tina was Japanese and her husband was a monk—Buddhist, I think, but never found out for sure. Mary was English, and I had no idea how Phyllis found them or how long they had worked there, but I got the impression it had been quite a long time.

"So there's six of us?" I asked Val.

"Seven."

I counted quickly—Tina and Mary, Val, Karen the wardrobe mistress, Maria, and me.

"You haven't met Ingrid. She's a college student and works part time on Phyllis's gag file."

The morning and afternoon breaks were the highlight of the day. Maria and I kept everyone informed of the latest plans—the agent had just called with an offer of a week in Chicago—and they told us the household activities—the gardener let the dogs out again, or Phyllis is having a birthday party for Cyd Charisse next week.

That first week Maria explained how everything worked in the office. She showed me stacks of 8x10 publicity photographs, some black and white and some in color.

"You take these when Phyllis is on the road. She will autograph them individually for people who request them." She then handed me a stack of postcards showing Phyllis in a short dress, with an elaborate feather headdress and holding a long cigarette holder. Later I found out that she didn't smoke—never had—the cigarette holder was a prop. "These are to give to fans. Phyllis doesn't autograph them."

Maria opened the closet door behind her. It was crammed with every kind of office need imaginable.

"This is what you will take with you on the road," she explained.

"All that?"

"No, of course not. I mean here is all that you will need to take in the office bag." She then pulled two white, hard-sided suitcases from the corner. "These are your office bags."

"A traveling office?" I wasn't at all sure I liked the looks of that.

"You will also take some of these books," Maria went on, gesturing to stacks of *Phyllis Diller's Housekeeping Hints* and *Phyllis Diller's Marriage Manual*. It seemed I was going to be taking an awful lot of stuff with me.

During the week, Maria showed me Phyllis's joke file, and I met Ingrid, the college student. Maria explained that whenever Phyllis came up with a new joke, she, Maria, would type it on a 3x5 index card and Ingrid then filed it in whatever category Phyllis had indicated. Sometimes jokes overlapped and Maria typed the joke on several different cards, and Ingrid filed them accordingly. It was quite a remarkable setup. So remarkable, it ended up in the Smithsonian.

Maria also explained how Phyllis got her bookings through the William Morris Agency, whom at the agency Phyllis dealt with, and how to handle the various kinds of phone calls. Most calls were business, but occasionally a fan would get hold of Phyllis's number. Those would be handled discreetly but firmly, Maria said.

Great, I thought. Discreet I could be. Firm would be another matter.

Maria went on to tell me about requests from organizations seeking items for celebrity auctions. I'd never heard of a celebrity auction, but apparently they were all the rage. Schools and charities requested items to auction off for fund-raisers. Maria would get all the particulars and ask Phyllis what, if anything, she would donate. Phyllis had a supply of her trademark cigarette holders just for that purpose, and sometimes she gave something more personal, such as a pair of boots or gloves that had seen better days. She usually autographed the item to increase its value.

"If anyone calls with a request, be sure to get all the information before you take it to Phyllis," Maria said.

I had this lesson driven home the following week when Phyllis's publicist, Frank, called to say that the Milk Board would pay Phyllis $50,000 to do a commercial. When I told Phyllis about it, she said, "What kind of commercial? Is it a billboard? Newspaper? Television? How long will it run? What market will it show in?" When I said I didn't know, she said, "You always need to get all the details." I never made that mistake again.

At the beginning of my second week they returned from London and I met Karen, a petite Hawaiian girl, for the first time. She had a no-nonsense attitude with definite ideas of how things should be done, and she quickly set me straight on the protocol of the household.

"You call Phyllis, Phyllis. Warde is Mr. Donovan, never

ever Mr. Diller. And some people think he's 'Fang,' but he's not."

Phyllis insisted Fang was purely fictional, but the household gossip had it that the character closely resembled Phyllis's first husband, Sherwood.

"If Warde tells you to do something, you check with Phyllis first," Karen continued. "Warde likes to stir the pot and cause trouble. Be careful of him."

"What about Phyllis?" I asked.

"You'll be fine as long as you do everything right."

Oh, swell.

"No, really," Karen went on. "Phyllis can be demanding. Her favorite word is 'perfect,' but you'll do fine."

I hoped she was right.

Karen, after explaining who was who, took me on a tour of the house. The place struck me as rather odd—one side had two stories, but the other side had only one. That wasn't apparent from the outside, but I had to wonder what the architect was thinking. Phyllis and Warde's bedroom was on the one-story side at the back of the house, which afforded absolute privacy—something Phyllis treasured.

Karen moved swiftly and with confidence as she showed me her domain—the wardrobe room right next to the bedroom. It was huge and meticulously arranged. "This side are the costumes. I hang them up by age, new ones in front. Phyllis's friend Omar makes them all."

It turned out that Omar's name was really Gloria, but Phyllis had dubbed her Omar the Tentmaker because of the A-line style of costumes Phyllis wore onstage. They could be said to vaguely resemble tents. Some of the costumes were outlandish while others were really beautiful. Of course, Phyllis always made them look outlandish when she added her jeweled dog collar, feathered headdress, and ankle-high boots.

"Phyllis designed the see-through hat boxes," Karen said as she motioned to the shelves above, which were lined with hats and headdresses.

Karen showed me the shelves with boots, and shallow drawers of gloves, cigarette holders, and the sparkly dog-collar necklaces Phyllis always wore onstage. Feather boas were arranged by color on their own padded hangers.

"These are street clothes," Karen said, turning to the other side of the room.

Really? Had me fooled. Some were normal clothes, such as dresses, blouses, and slacks, but some were flowing, flowering caftans and sparkly dresses that surely Phyllis could've worn onstage. There were also hangers with the white-on-white outfits Phyllis wore around the house. Sometimes when she wanted to go out shopping or make some other quick trip, she would add a white hood that covered her hair, and large sunglasses. She considered this a disguise, but it actually drew more attention than if she'd just looked like herself. And, of course, there was no way to disguise the laugh. And Phyllis liked to laugh!

As we went through the wardrobe, Karen straightened a dress here, rearranged a drawer there, and switched some of the shoes and boots around to her satisfaction. Sometimes after Phyllis had been rummaging for something to wear, Karen would spend thirty minutes putting everything back the way it should be.

Finally, Karen motioned to the back of the room. "Here are her evening clothes."

Oh my gosh. I stood and stared. Long gowns and short cocktail dresses, beaded and plain, elegant and kitschy covered the entire back wall. In addition, Phyllis had an array of wraps—coats and shawls—and finally a rack that held her many fur coats, from short car coats to dress-length mink coats in several shades, and a floor-length white ermine and an elegant gray chinchilla. The chinchilla fur was so thick and soft that touching it made me feel as though I had a handful of whipped cream. Phyllis had a lot of beautiful clothes. Everything smelled faintly of her special perfume. The wardrobe room had plenty of light and was quite large, but even so it seemed oppressive and I was glad to leave.

Karen flipped off the banks of lights, and we proceeded down the hallway toward the front of the house past Val's office. Val ran the household and saw to all the shopping, cleaning, and everything else that needed to be done, as I already knew. I found Val a bit odd. She always seemed a little nervous. As I came to know everyone, I realized she was the only one in the house who really got along with Warde.

Karen relied on Val to get the clothes to the cleaners when we got back from a trip, and Karen always checked to make sure everything was clean and ready to go for the next time. Karen herself did any mending of costumes, replacing missing buttons, sequins, or alterations that Phyllis requested. She put the gloves back in the right drawer, arranged by color, and made sure that any that had gotten soiled were cleaned before they were put away. Same for all the costumes, shoes, and other accessories.

After Val's office, Karen showed me the long, screened-in Calvin Coolidge Porch, which ran along the single-story side of the house by the master bedroom. Phyllis loved to sit out there on pleasant days and often did her work—studying scripts, writing material, reviewing letters and contracts—in that somewhat remote and quiet setting that overlooked the wide, green lawn.

The front of the house had the huge living room, which was filled with vases of red roses—her favorite. The day of my interview, I'd gone over to smell them. I was startled to find they were artificial. They were so perfectly crafted that they really, truly, looked real. The living room had a high ceiling and stained- and leaded-glass windows, and a cozy alcove with two small settees. It was rather old-fashioned and sweet.

We passed through the dining room and billiards room and ended up in the bright-red kitchen. Karen poured us each a cup of coffee and we settled in the small dinette where we had our breaks.

"So, what do you think?"

"It's a gorgeous house," I said. It was very open, with lots of windows and decorated in an eclectic style—lots of antiques but also the occasional strange little doodad that had no doubt struck Phyllis's fancy and she'd put on display. I had seen nothing cheap or jarring, however, and somehow it all came together.

"This is going to sound odd," I said as I poured cream into my coffee, "but there is something a little spooky back there."

"You mean the wardrobe room?"

I nodded.

"It's haunted."

I stared at Karen for a moment to see if she was laughing. She wasn't.

"I don't believe in ghosts," I said perhaps a little more forcefully than I needed to.

She shrugged.

"I don't, either," she said, "but everybody knows there's something strange with that room."

From that time on, I avoided it as much as possible. I told myself it was only because of the massive racks of clothes, with the hats on the shelf above, that made it look almost like there were people in there. Of course, there weren't. Not people and not ghosts, either. Still, I always quickened my pace as I walked past it.

4

The next day I began working with Phyllis, glad to learn that Warde had stopped in New York on his way back from London. At least I didn't have to get used to both of them at the same time.

Shortly before noon, which was shortly after she got up, Phyllis buzzed me on the intercom. "Come down and bring your note pad," she instructed. I took the back stairway just outside the office into the anteroom off the master bedroom. There was no door between the anteroom and the bedroom, and I hesitated.

"Come in," Phyllis called. She was seated on the edge of the bed wearing her "uniform"—a white, short-sleeved shirt, white slacks, and white ballet slippers. Stacks of paper, letters, notes, and pictures were scattered about the room. It would have been a beautiful bedroom if it weren't so cluttered. Windows looked out on the garden, and in an alcove stood a harpsichord.

Hardly ever see those anymore, I thought. Karen told me that Phyllis had studied to be a concert pianist. I sat in the small chair Phyllis indicated.

"You've met everyone," Phyllis said. It was half question and half statement.

I nodded.

"Here's my schedule. Maria keeps it up-to-date." She reached down and plucked a paper off the closest pile. "Now, let's see. This is a little out-of-date. We just got back from London . . ." She crossed off the top item on the schedule ". . . and Saturday we leave for Pittsburgh. I play the Holiday House there for a week. Tomorrow I'm taping at ABC. This date in Dallas has been canceled." She crossed out another portion of the schedule and handed it to me. "Ask Maria for a new one."

I then spent an hour trailing her around the house trying to remember the mixture of instructions, some to do with work, some to do with family.

"My son, Perry, lives with me, as well as Warde's two boys, Shane and Todd. My daughter, Susie, lives here, too. She has the Abraham Lincoln Suite."

Phyllis had named many of the rooms. She'd christened the living room the Bob Hope Salon, obviously because of the huge portrait; the screened-in sun porch was the Calvin Coolidge Porch because she had furnished it with cool, white wicker; a hall closet that Phyllis had converted into a private phone booth she had dubbed the John Wilkes Booth; and at the back of the house was a sort of rumpus room all done in red-and-white stripes and sporting a soda fountain—the Doris Day Room.

Phyllis rattled off a list of people I would be dealing with: her agent, Fred; her publicist, Frank; her attorney, Mr. B (whom I'd already "met" over the phone); her travel agent, Jimmy; and the names of her designer, decorator, children who weren't living there, and a dozen others. I scribbled frantically. She also confirmed something Karen had told me: "If Warde tells you to do anything, you check with me first. He sometimes likes to think he's my manager, but he's not."

I nodded, perhaps too enthusiastically.

"There is one other thing," she said as she sat down and motioned me to do likewise. "He often does things that are annoying, and he may try to interfere with your work. If he does, you come tell me. But if it comes to a showdown between the two of you, I'll side with him. You are my secretary, but Warde is my husband."

At least I knew where I stood and was glad that she had laid it out in the open. I realized that he was in a difficult position. Not many men like to live off of a woman, but she wanted a husband who would travel with her, so it was impossible for him to have a "regular" job. I suppose that throwing his weight around made him feel important. At that moment, however, I was glad he wasn't around. He was going to meet us in Pittsburgh.

By the end of the first week, I had a hazy picture of what Phyllis Diller was really like. She was smart and focused. She was exacting but not unreasonable, nor did she have a temper. I figured that someone who had made it to the top of that strange business and could keep her humanity, her perspective, and her dignity had earned every right to be demanding. I had no problem with that.

She was also something of a paradox. Although she seemed determined to establish a definite employer-employee relationship, at break time she often came into the kitchen and told jokes until we were all in stitches. She particularly liked jokes about food. My favorite was: "My idea of the perfect hostess is one who can convince her dinner guests that caraway seeds have legs!" Then she would laugh that full-throated, raucous laugh, and how could we help but all laugh with her? However, I had the impression of someone who, in spite of her fame and her wealth, was perhaps a little lonely.

5

Phyllis liked to get her work done in the morning. Usually, sometime around 10:30 or 11:00, she'd summon me by saying, "Come down and bring your notebook." From the beginning, she delegated the routine correspondence, and it wasn't long before she would simply hand me a contract and say, "Make the arrangements."

Some things Maria took care of, but I personally talked to the people we'd be dealing with. I wanted to confirm rehearsals and publicity appearances and nail down details. The first person I'd call was Phyllis's agent to find out anything that might not be obvious.

"Hey," he told me one time, "that promoter is going to try to get Phyllis to do some personal appearances. That's not in the contract. Tell him no." Or, "There's a radio station that does promos for the theater and Phyllis has agreed to record something for them. Give them a call when you get settled and Phyllis can do that over the phone."

While Maria talked to the travel agent making airline and hotel reservations, I'd call the limo company both in L.A. and at our destination. In New York and Chicago, Phyllis not only used a particular limo service but had a favorite driver that I learned to ask for. Phyllis told me that small cities and towns often did not have limousine companies, so I should contact the local mortuary—they had limos for funerals and were perfectly happy to rent them out.

"Be sure not to book the hearse!" Phyllis once said, then erupted into laughter.

My first trip with her would be to Philadelphia. While Maria talked to the travel agent, I called the limo company in L.A. and asked what time they should pick us up to get to the airport on time.

Phyllis had come up to the office for some reason—something she almost never did.

"No! You don't ask them. You tell them when to be here."

I was flummoxed because I had no idea how long it would take to drive from Phyllis's house to the airport. This was her regular limo company, so I figured they would know. Thank goodness the dispatcher on the other end of the line heard Phyllis's voice and quietly said to me, "Eight A.M. You need to leave the house at eight."

"We need to leave the house at eight in the morning. Have the limo here at seven forty-five," I said, repeating it back to her.

Phyllis nodded approvingly as she left the room. Maria looked across the desk at me with an encouraging smile. Maria adored Phyllis but also knew that occasionally, very seldom but once in a long while, Phyllis actually could be wrong.

In spite of that aberration when she expected me to tell someone something I couldn't have known, it was obvious that Phyllis had a sharp mind, a good business sense, and a phenomenal memory. Sometimes on the road a person would come up to her and say, "Do you remember me?" She would look at him for a moment, then say,

"Magic Circle Theater, Sacramento. You were the sound man."

On days when she was home, she often met friends for lunch. Phyllis had many friends; she went out to lunch a lot.

6

The first week Phyllis was back, she had a television taping at ABC. Karen drove the Rolls Royce, and we were barely out of the driveway when Phyllis handed me a contract. She pointed to her signature.

"I want you to learn to write my name," she said. "I don't have time to sign everything. I want you to do it for me."

"Contracts?" I asked.

"Everything."

I got busy tracing her name, then opened my shorthand notebook to a clean page and started writing "Phyllis Diller." By the time we got to the studio, I had two pages full. I showed my forgeries to Phyllis.

"Not bad," she said, "but the *h* doesn't have a loop and there's no tail on the *s*. Make the *l*'s a little closer together."

The guard waved us through and Karen let us off at the back entrance. We hurried through hallways with

Phyllis occasionally waving to someone. I was amazed that someone four inches shorter than I could walk so much faster. A quick scurry was her usual pace. Fortunately, Phyllis knew where she was going and in a few minutes we were in her dressing room. I thought I had a good sense of direction, but I was totally turned around. Karen had obviously done this before, since she turned up a few minutes later.

While Karen arranged the costumes and Phyllis got ready for makeup, I realized there was nothing for me to do there.

"Why don't you go out front and watch?" Phyllis said.

I slipped out onto the set. The mélange of cameras and lights, "grips" (the stagehands who moved the equipment), electricians, script girls, directors, and "gofers" fascinated me. I couldn't imagine anything coherent emerging from that mayhem.

The sets were merely "flats," a wall with a door or a window in it, propped up in back. Two or three of these made up a room, which was open on the fourth side for the camera. Overhead, the lights and microphones dangled out of the camera's view. I found a place to sit out of everybody's way and watched as the mayhem gradually resolved itself into order. Taping Phyllis's segment took most of the day. At lunch there was a huge buffet of cold cuts and fruit. Karen and I sat at a table with Louis Jordan and George Maharis, whom I'd had a crush on since the first time I saw him on *Route 66*. We had a pleasant and casual chat as if we were really friends.

Wow, I thought, *this is the big time!*

It was nearly five o'clock by the time we left the studio, and I was glad that Phyllis required only one day of shooting. Between trying to figure out what was going on and staying out of everybody's way, I was exhausted, although I hadn't done a lick of work. I did have several more pages filled with "Phyllis Diller," though. Phyllis glanced at them and told me I was ready to start signing things.

The next day, Maria and I packed for the trip to Pittsburgh. "Here's the briefcase. I put in a new shorthand notebook, pens, the contract for the club, Phyllis's address book, autographed pictures, and Phyllis Diller postcards." It seemed excessive to me, but what did I know?

"On this side," Maria continued, "is the expanded schedule. It lists all the interviews, contact numbers, rehearsal and show times. Now let me show you the office bag." I couldn't imagine we'd need anything more, but apparently we did.

Maria had packed the office bag with staplers and staple removers, Scotch tape, boxes of paper clips, dozens of pens in different colors, scratch pads, pencils, a pencil sharpener, an extra ribbon for my typewriter ("just in case," she said), several large, yellow legal pads, and anything else necessary to set up an instant office any place on the planet. It also had two dozen of Phyllis's new book, *Housekeeping Hints.*

"The office bag you can check," Maria told me.

Well, thank heaven for that. In addition to the briefcase and my purse, I would also have to carry my electric portable typewriter. I felt like a porter. *Is this the glamour Mr. B talked about?*

Maria handed me the petty-cash purse. Just then Karen came up from the wardrobe room. "Well, we got the costumes done," she said.

"What were you doing with the costumes?"

"Accessorizing."

"Like how?"

"You know, picking out the gloves, the boots, the headdress that goes with each dress."

I hadn't thought about it, but of course there would be different gloves and shoes for every costume. Finding and choosing just the right pair of gloves or headdress would take time. No wonder Karen was so fussy about everything being in its proper place.

Eyeing the petty-cash purse she said, "We need to go to the bank and get some money. Two hundred should do it. Here, write a check."

"Why do we need two hundred dollars?" I asked.

"Money for tips, taxis, and if Phyllis wants us to buy something."

I wrote a check for $200, signed Phyllis's name, and Karen took me to the local bank where Phyllis had her account. Karen introduced me to the tellers and the vice president. No one questioned the signature on the check.

Back at the house I made last-minute calls to the limousine service in Los Angeles confirming the limo and "baggage wagon" for 7:45 A.M. Phyllis's travel agent called to confirm the limo at the airport in Pittsburgh. He also said a passenger service representative from the airline would be at the airports in L.A. and Pittsburgh, and assured me he'd made hotel reservations for Karen and me. Phyllis and Warde were staying in an apartment that Phyllis owned.

The next morning my dad drove me to the house so I wouldn't have to leave my car parked in Phyllis's driveway while we were away. Until I had a steady job and income, I did not want to start looking for my own place. My parents and I had a good relationship, and after seeing me only once in those nearly five years I'd been overseas, they were delighted to have me at home. We all knew it was temporary, but for the time being it was pretty comfortable. I sure didn't expect my father to drive me to Phyllis's every time we went out of town, but he liked to know where I would be working. Even though I was twenty-eight years old, I was still his "little girl."

When we arrived, Karen was stacking luggage on the front porch. "Are you early, or am I late?" I asked as I jumped out of the car.

"Early. Good thing, too. Omar just left—they've been playing cards and yakking all night. I had to finish the packing."

Normally, Phyllis did her own packing.

The "baggage wagon," which turned out to be a second limousine, arrived shortly and I realized the necessity of having a separate vehicle for the luggage. Karen and I formed sort of a bucket brigade; she handed me the bags off the porch and I passed them on to the driver, who stashed them in the trunk.

"Hey, this one's empty!" I said.

"No, it's the feathers."

So there was a bag with feather boas and headdresses, two wig boxes for the fright wigs Phyllis wore onstage, two suitcases with costumes, Phyllis's two regular suitcases, a bag with things for Warde, who was meeting us there, my office bag, and a "kitchen bag." The kitchen bag was heavy and when I saw what was inside, I understood. There was a hot plate, pans, utensils, cutlery, assorted herbs and spices, cans of soup and some crackers. Added to that were Karen's suitcase, which matched Phyllis's, and mine, which didn't.

I'd learned more about Phyllis Diller since the day I said "yes" to the lady at the employment agency. The traveling kitchen, I realized, probably reflected an uncertain childhood during the Depression. Phyllis had been an only child of older parents and evidently learned to be self-reliant at an early age. Also, times were tough during her first marriage to a husband who couldn't or wouldn't hold a job. There were days when she didn't know where they'd get money to buy food for the growing family. Although she was no Scarlett O'Hara, I'd guessed that she had promised herself she and her family would never go hungry again.

Warde was another dish of fish entirely. Karen told me he came from a wealthy, prestigious family. His brother was Chairman of the Board at Disney Studios. Perhaps my first impression of him had been wrong, I told myself as we continued to hand suitcases down to the limo driver.

Phyllis, somewhat bleary-eyed, came outside to see how we were doing. When she saw my suitcase, she turned back into the house and in just a moment was back with one of hers. "Use this," she said. "With all the traveling we do, you'll wear yours out in no time. Besides, it's easier to pick them out when they all match." There wasn't time to repack my suitcase right there on the front porch, so I sent her huge, red-plaid suitcase home with my dad, but used it on all the trips after that.

I'd asked my dad to wait until we were on our way. I don't know quite why, but I just wanted to make sure everything was going to happen the way I thought it would. When Phyllis saw me handing the suitcase to him, she waved us both over.

"Phyllis, may I present my father?" I asked.

"I'm very pleased to meet you, Miss Diller," my father said as she held out her hand. My father was a proper English gentleman and even at this early hour on a Saturday morning, he was wearing a suit and tie. Phyllis was properly impressed. She liked him even better when I told her that we had a Chickering grand piano and he played classical music.

Score one for our side, Dad.

I had an odd introduction to traveling with Phyllis Diller. The usual arrangement had Phyllis and Warde in first class, while Karen and I went coach. However, Warde had gone directly to Philadelphia from New York, where he'd been since Phyllis got back from England. Phyllis never sat alone, so I got to enjoy first class while Karen sat in coach. I had never flown first class before. The crew recognized Phyllis and catered to her outrageously, filling her glass with champagne whenever it was less than half full.

What is this? Some kind of game? We hadn't been in the air more than forty minutes and she'd consumed the better part of a bottle. I became uneasy when after the third refill Phyllis decided to show me the contents of her purse. Like the Queen of England, there was no need for her to carry her own handbag, but she preferred it that way.

"Do you want to see my jewelry?" she asked with the solemn air of a kindergartner holding a pet frog for inspection. She didn't wait for an answer but opened her large tapestry bag and pulled out a smaller one.

"Here," she said, unzipping what looked like a cosmetic bag and fishing out a ring. "It's a cabochon ruby. Thirty-five carats." She dropped it into my hand. It felt heavy and inappropriately large for her small hand. The ruby was set in gold and ringed with diamonds.

"Look at this," she commanded, pulling the next item from her bag. "It's my diamond." It sure was—it was actually half a dozen large diamonds of different cuts and sizes that looked as though they had haphazardly fallen into a delicate setting of gold. "Each stone has a story," she said. "This one is from my mother's wedding ring, and this one was given to me by Omar. It was from her engagement ring." Phyllis continued pointing out each stone and its significance, then dropped it into my lap beside the ruby. (Both rings were stolen a year later when Phyllis left them in the restroom of an airplane.)

On she went pulling rings, brooches, and bracelets from her bag and holding them up for me to see, then dropping them in my hands. I'd spread a napkin across my lap and placed each one in it as Phyllis delved back into her bag for more. I was getting nervous. I didn't think we were going to be robbed at gunpoint in an airplane, but what happened if we hit an air pocket and all those magnificent baubles went flying? When she reached the end, she scooped them all up and stuffed them back in her bag. At least I knew why she insisted on carrying her own purse. And why it was so heavy.

7

We arrived in Pittsburgh midafternoon. Rehearsal was at 6:00 p.m., the first of two shows at 8:00 p.m. Rather than a limo, a Chrysler Town Car was waiting at the airport. Because all of our luggage wouldn't fit in the trunk, Karen and I sat in the front seat, each holding a wig box. Phyllis was in the back with three large suitcases. I sighed with relief when the driver dropped me at the Hilton. Karen and Phyllis went on to the nearby apartment where Warde was waiting.

"We'll be back for you in a few minutes," Phyllis called as the car pulled away. I dashed inside to check in.

"I'm sorry, ma'am, but your rooms aren't quite ready," the desk clerk said. He didn't sound sorry in the slightest.

"I'm in a hurry. I have to leave again in a few minutes."

"Hmm." He flipped through some pages. "Did you specifically want the tower?"

"No. It doesn't matter. Anything."

"Two rooms, right?

"Yes. Two."

"You want them close?"

"I don't care. Just two rooms!" I felt sweat running down my back.

After flipping through a few more pages and placing a call, he handed me a couple of keys.

"They're not together," he said.

"Fine." The porter had returned to the bell desk and was summoned. He took our bags up and I directed the disposition of each—my white suitcase and the office bag in one room, Karen's big plaid suitcase in the room down the hall. I barely had time to use the bathroom and run a comb through my hair. I rushed downstairs.

The doorman greeted me with a big smile.

"Are you Miss Diller's secretary?" he asked.

I nodded.

"They just left," he said.

"They what?"

"They were here and said they couldn't wait. They went on to the club but said you didn't have to bother to come out."

"They left me here?"

"Guess you have the night off."

"Really? You're not joking?" I had a horrible sinking feeling. What had she meant by "don't bother to come out"? Was I fired? Was that the equivalent of "take the next plane home"? Besides the anxiety, I was terribly disappointed. I'd been looking forward to the excitement of the theater and seeing Phyllis onstage.

I had learned a lot about the famous Phyllis Diller in the past couple of weeks. Each friend I told about my new job immediately began telling me about Phyllis Diller. From each one, I heard something different: her movies with Bob Hope; her appearances on the *Ed Sullivan Show*; that she had started show business at the age of forty; that she was the first, best, and funniest stand-up comedienne ever! Everyone told me how incredibly funny she was and how incredibly lucky I was to be working for her. However, at that moment I didn't feel lucky at all. I wondered if I would be one of her short-lived secretaries, sent home in disgrace on the next plane.

"Is there a bus that goes out to the Holiday House?" I asked.

"Bless you, now," he laughed. "That's nearly thirty miles away. Even if there were, it would take you a long time. No, there's no way to get there except by car or taxi."

"Well, please call me a taxi," I said and for a fleeting moment thought he was going to say, "All right, you're a taxi," but he didn't. I wondered if I would have enough money for the fare, then remembered the $200 petty cash. I would pay it back later.

It was a long drive and I worried the whole way. Perhaps I should have stayed at the hotel and had dinner, written a few letters, practiced writing "Phyllis Diller" a few hundred times more. I realized, once I had a few minutes to catch my breath, I could have had the bellman stash the suitcases and checked into our rooms later. (Afterward I was glad I hadn't done that because we didn't get home until midnight.) I also realized I could have phoned out to the club and seen what the message meant. Feeling miserable, I huddled in the taxi and hoped I still had a job.

The Holiday House was a large motor inn with a showroom. At the front desk a clerk directed me to suite 223. With more trepidation than I had felt since I'd learned I was going to a job interview with Phyllis Diller, I knocked on the door. When the door opened, I had an almost overwhelming urge to turn and run. There stood Warde wearing nothing but skimpy briefs. We stared at each other for several seconds. I wondered if he remembered me. He did.

"They're in the other room," he said finally and waved casually toward a door. I slipped past him as quickly as possible. I was not used to seeing strange men walking about nearly nude. (When I told Karen, she couldn't resist saying, "They don't come any stranger than Warde.")

The scene in the next room wasn't a great deal better. Phyllis sat at the dressing table putting on her stage makeup, wearing nothing but panty hose and bra. Thank heaven Karen was fully clothed. Phyllis and Karen looked surprised to see me.

"Didn't you get my message?" Phyllis asked.

"Yes, but I didn't know what else to do."

"Well, there's nothing for you to do right now. Why don't you go wait in the other room." Her tone was not unfriendly, just practical.

At that moment, Warde came in and pulled a short robe out of the closet. He slipped into it and checked himself out in the mirror. The thing barely covered his butt, but it was certainly an improvement over the skimpy briefs.

Warde turned to go back into the living room and I followed. He settled into a chair and started watching TV. He made no attempt at conversation, thank God. I sat stiffly on the couch and grabbed the only thing to read—a hotel guide for the eastern half of the United States—and studied it as if I were getting ready for a final exam.

Finally, the door to the adjoining room opened. "Honey, don't you think you'd better get ready?" Phyllis asked. It turned out that Warde was a singer and her opening act.

Warde got up and I averted my eyes as he passed in front of me on his way to the dressing room. A few minutes later, the adjoining door opened again. Karen poked her head out and said to me, "C'mon in."

Warde was just leaving, heading downstairs. He had changed into a beautifully cut suit and a white silk shirt open at the collar. He cut a very dashing figure. I later found out that he loved shopping at expensive men's stores in Beverly Hills. This was certainly not some off-the-rack suit. He looked elegant and every bit the star.

Phyllis still had on her underwear, although she had completed her makeup and donned her wig. I sat quietly while Phyllis scanned her correspondence and Karen rearranged some of the accessories to her satisfaction.

Through the speaker in the dressing room we listened as Warde went through his act. I perked up, surprised to hear a beautiful tenor voice as he began "On a Clear Day." I wondered why he had never made it in the big time. He had no doubt been extremely handsome twenty years earlier and still looked good.

After about twenty minutes, Phyllis put her papers down. Evidently that was the signal to get moving.

"Robin, will you hand me Phyllis's costume?" Karen asked as she selected a pair of gloves from the array on the dressing table. "It's there in the closet."

When I handed over the sequined dress, I understood why Phyllis waited until the last minute to put it on—it must have weighed twenty pounds. Once Phyllis was dressed, Karen gave her the matching gloves and the famous prop cigarette holder. Warde was nearing the end of his act, and I trailed Phyllis and Karen down the stairs and stood in the wings while he took his bows and the stage manager introduced Phyllis.

"C'mon," Karen said, once Phyllis was onstage. "Let's sit out front and watch the show. We don't want to go back up to the suite."

Oh, yeah. Just the idea of sitting in a room with Warde for the next forty-five minutes gave me the willies. Karen led the way out a side door and we found some seats toward the back.

As we watched Phyllis onstage, I laughed so hard that I gasped for breath. Karen chuckled occasionally.

"Don't you like her act?" I managed to ask.

"Yeah," Karen answered with a quick smile, "but I've heard it a couple hundred times."

When it ended, we slipped backstage to escort Phyllis up to the suite. Phyllis ordered dinner for all of us. I was glad since I had already realized the $10 per diem wasn't going to cover much if I had to eat in hotels.

We finished dinner, went through the second show and headed for home. The limo dropped Karen and me off at the hotel before it took Phyllis and Warde to the apartment. Karen came to my room and even though it was late, we settled in to talk. Karen had worked for Phyllis for over a year. She originally got the job when her friend, Ruth, started as Phyllis's secretary. Ruth had quit after only a short time; she had no patience with Warde.

"So, did Phyllis get Ruth through an agency?" I asked.

"No, Ruth is from New York. She's a friend of Phyllis's lawyer. I think you're the first secretary Phyllis got through an agency."

"How do entertainers usually get their secretaries?"

Karen shrugged. "All I know is that Phyllis always found someone who knew someone who wanted a job. The housekeeper's niece or something like that. It never worked out. Take Louise, for instance—the one that left in New Orleans. She was a great secretary but hated to travel. She got ulcers. The one before that loved traveling and being Phyllis Diller's secretary, but she didn't want to work. One day I discovered she was throwing all the mail in the wastebasket. I told Phyllis and that was the end of her. The one before her was real young. The only thing she wanted was to go to bed with Perry. So, anyway," Karen concluded, "Phyllis decided to go to an agency and get a professional."

I stopped myself just in time from asking who that was. She was talking about me!

"I couldn't believe it tonight when I went downstairs and the doorman told me you had already left!" I said.

"Phyllis likes punctuality."

"Really?" I said, thinking of the one o'clock interview that had begun at four o'clock.

"Actually, Phyllis was impressed that you'd taken the initiative to come out to the club. She said it showed dedication."

"So what am I going to be doing out there?"

"Oh, I'm sure Phyllis will want to dictate letters, go over stuff. It's just that opening night we're getting everything set up. I'll bet you'll have plenty to do the rest of the time. By the way, take the cab fare out of petty cash," Karen said.

"I can't do that. It wasn't Phyllis's fault that I wasn't downstairs."

"Well, it wasn't yours, either. Don't pay for that out of your own pocket. That's part of miscellaneous expenses." I argued halfheartedly, but then acquiesced.

"Hey," I said, wanting to change the subject, "I was really impressed with Warde's act. He's a terrific singer. Why isn't he better known?"

"You'll see." Karen refused to say more.

Two nights later, we were in the suite, Phyllis half-dressed and going over the next day's schedule, when her head shot up.

"He's doing it!" she barked, staring at the speaker. "Karen, quick!"

Karen was ahead of her, holding out the costume for Phyllis to step into. The dog collar came next, then they were out the door, Phyllis pulling on her gloves as she pounded down the stairs with Karen close behind, grasping the cigarette holder.

I had been taken totally off guard. Warde had been onstage only a few minutes.

"What's happening?" I whispered to Karen when I caught up.

"That's his closing number," she said and nodded toward the stage.

"How come?"

She shrugged. Then Warde came offstage, heading for the stairs, and the stage manager introduced Phyllis. As soon as Phyllis took the stage, Karen grabbed me and headed outside.

"We don't want to be around for the fireworks," she said. We went to the coffee shop and ordered dinner.

"Why did he stop in the middle of his act?" I asked as soon as we were seated.

Karen shook her head. "Phyllis calls it 'attitude.' He acts as though these people are a bunch of yokels, and it comes across."

I remembered his sneer and condescending attitude the first day I met him.

"He doesn't like them, and they don't like him," Karen added. "A couple of times he's actually been booed off the stage."

Our dinners came. Karen dug into her spaghetti, but I'd lost my appetite and simply toyed with my food. *This isn't good. Not good at all.*

We prudently waited until after Warde had gone onstage for the second show before returning to the suite. Phyllis was in a towering rage. She sat at the dressing table, picking up makeup bottles and slamming them down so hard I thought they might break. She got up and paced the room. "That's it!" she snapped. She paused midpace and turned to look at me. I cringed as anger radiated from her. "That's the last time he does this to me. He's never going to work with me again. I've told him and told him." She drew her mouth into a thin line. I wondered if she might hurl one of those bottles across the room, but I realized she had a tight rein on her emotions.

"Do you know how hard it is to follow something like that?" she said and continued to glare at me. I gulped and shook my head.

"Do you know what that does to an audience?" she persisted.

Rhetorical question, I told myself, and kept my mouth shut.

"By the time I get out there, they are so hostile that I have to work twice as hard. I might as well throw away the first half of my act—it takes that long to bring them around. The opening act is supposed to warm up the audience!"

She resumed pacing. "By the time I get out there, those people should be relaxed and in a good mood. That's what they paid for!"

She stopped and sat down. Her shoulders sagged. There was near total silence in the dressing room for several minutes. I could still hear Warde over the speakers, but they'd been turned way down.

"Here's your dress," Karen said.

"Do you know what else this means?" Phyllis asked quietly as she stood up and stepped into the costume. "This means that I have to be ready half an hour early every night and sit around sweating, just in case he decides to quit." I wondered how she'd ever be able to go onstage and be funny.

She sighed. "We might as well go on down. I don't want to have to race down those stairs again. One of these days I'm going to trip and break my neck."

When we got backstage, Phyllis stood in a corner by herself, absently returning smiles from the stage crew and obviously psyching herself.

Warde finished—he did his whole act. The introduction played and Phyllis dashed onstage. A minute later she was telling "the truth" about her dress: "I used to be a lampshade in a whorehouse. Couldn't get one of the good jobs. Listen, you think my legs are skinny? Colonel Sanders is crazy about them . . ." She laughed and cavorted, telling silly stories and having a wonderful time. The audience loved every minute.

On the ride home, Warde was determined to make Phyllis understand what had compelled him to walk offstage. Phyllis kept saying, "We'll talk about it when we get home," but he insisted on explaining to her how bad the audience was, how they didn't pay attention, didn't appreciate talent, how somebody like him just couldn't deal with it and on and on.

"Warde, we will discuss this when we're alone," she repeated.

Warde pretended to be startled, as if he hadn't realized there were other people in the car. He tried hard to pretend that the hired help didn't exist. He referred to this as having "class." I came to find out he talked about it often, trying to convince somebody that he had some.

If he weren't such a nasty human being, I decided, I could almost have felt sorry for him. But he was, and I didn't.

8

Outside of the Big Fight, which they made up, there were two other incidents that week that stand out in my mind. Phyllis was scheduled to be the half-time entertainment for a football game in Three Rivers Stadium. At Phyllis's request, Warde had been asked to sing the national anthem for the game's opening. It turned into a mortifying embarrassment when halfway through *The Star Spangled Banner* he forgot the words. He ad-libbed something that at least rhymed and hoped nobody would notice. Afterward, he brushed it off, saying he hadn't sung it for ages.

The other incident occurred during a radio talk show, where people phoned in. Most of the callers said more or less the same thing—how much they liked Phyllis—or asked predictable questions, such as how did she get into show business? Or did she write her own material? One call, however, shook everyone up. A man said he wanted to talk to Phyllis Diller. Everything was on speaker phones so Phyllis and the DJ could be on at the same time and the caller's voice could be heard by everyone in the studio.

"I'm here," chirped Phyllis.

"I just wanted you to know," the man said, "that I'm going to kill you."

Immediately the DJ pushed the disconnect button and announced it was time for a commercial break. It was a live show, so it had a ten-second delay and the call never went out over the air, but Phyllis had become ashen and visibly shaken.

Although it shocked everyone, the DJ apparently had experienced that kind of thing before. He poured Phyllis a fresh glass of water and kept up a smooth flow of soothing chatter. The break ended quickly and in another ninety seconds they were back on the air. He thanked Phyllis for coming down to the studio and reminded the listeners that she would be at the Holiday House Supper Club for three more nights.

As we left the studio, the staff was reassuring and thoughtful. One of them went downstairs and hailed us a cab. It was my first introduction to the pathetic losers who got their thrills from threatening celebrities.

We went from the cab to the elevator and into the apartment without seeing anyone. Phyllis went straight to the kitchen.

"I'm cooking dinner for you," she announced. "Do you like garlic?"

Phyllis got out her knives and started chopping cloves and immediately the room filled with the pungent scent of garlic. I realized that it didn't matter whether I liked garlic or not. That's what we were having.

Warde came in while she was filling a huge pan with water. "How'd it go?" he asked, picking up a lime and cutting it in half.

"Fine, Warde."

He added ice cubes to a glass and reached for the gin. "Did you remember to plug the Holiday House?"

Phyllis didn't respond, and I picked up the three-day-old newspaper from the table.

The door opened and Karen walked in. "Perry called," she told Phyllis.

"Fine. I'll call him later. I'm making spaghetti," Phyllis said and tossed the chopped garlic—lots of it—into a small sauté pan and added a cube of butter.

"Hand me that spaghetti," she said to Warde.

"Wouldn't you rather have a drink?" he asked and attempted to hand her the gin on the rocks instead.

"Not before the show!"

I continued to study the newspaper.

"The spaghetti, Warde."

Warde set down his drink, tore open the package and handed it to Phyllis. She dumped the entire contents into the boiling water. Warde picked up his drink and went back to wherever he'd come from.

When the pasta was done, Phyllis tossed everything together, added a bit of salt and pepper, and divided it among four plates.

"Warde, dinner," Phyllis called. He appeared promptly, *sans* drink, and we sat down to the table. We were all quiet as we slurped up the garlic spaghetti. We didn't leave a scrap.

The chopping of the garlic must've been therapeutic because by the time we got to the theater, Phyllis had returned to normal.

Nothing untoward happened for the rest of the run. Warde performed his act according to plan, the audiences continued to love Phyllis, and I spent afternoons at the apartment taking dictation.

Two days before Phyllis's show closed at the Holiday House, Phyllis told me to put together a tip list. "You need to get the names and the correct spelling; that's very important. I want to acknowledge everyone I worked with."

Karen coached me on who should receive a tip from Phyllis and it was indeed everyone. I wrote down the names of the limo driver, the stage manager, the spotlight operator, the sound man, the doorman, and everyone else who'd done anything for Phyllis while we were there.

"Do you have the books?" she asked.

Ah! That's why Maria had put two dozen copies of Housekeeping Hints *in the office bag.*

Phyllis autographed them individually and usually added a cute comment. Some people, like the stage manager, got cash. She told me who and how much, and I put it in an envelope along with the note from her.

When it came time to leave, I almost panicked over the preparations. I checked and double-checked on the limousines on both ends, and confirmed that a passenger service rep would be in Pittsburgh and L.A. At the airport the porter argued about how many bags we were allowed, but when he found out the luggage belonged to Phyllis Diller, he just smiled and wrote out the baggage tags. A large tip didn't hurt, either. Phyllis's policy was to tip double the going rate. Many other celebrities weren't so generous. I appreciated her largess. It certainly made life easier for me. I just wished she had the same attitude toward her own staff.

By the time my dad picked me up at Phyllis's house in Brentwood at 5:00, we'd worked more than a twelve-hour day. We drove Karen home and on the way filled my dad in on the details of the trip. He raised his eyebrows at Warde's behavior and let me know that he wasn't at all sure this was the best of all possible situations for his daughter.

"Are we coming to work tomorrow?" I asked Karen as we pulled up to her building.

"Sure, why not?"

"Well, you know, we did work both Saturday and Sunday, and I just thought that we've put in a couple of twelve-hour days so we might, you know, get a day off?" I didn't know why I should feel hesitant about asking. It seemed as if we were always working, especially Karen, who continually maintained the costumes, mended torn gloves, glued a broken cigarette holder. And if she wasn't doing that, she was grocery shopping or doing other errands for Phyllis and Warde. Sometimes Phyllis did some of her own shopping, but most often Karen did it in her so-called free time.

I'd spend my mornings typing the letters Phyllis had dictated the afternoon before. In addition to that, I took all of Phyllis's phone calls. The only calls that went directly to her were family or friends. Promoters and people seeking interviews called for her at the theater. I returned the calls in the morning, setting up tentative appointments for her to approve. I also talked to fans, promising an autographed picture to be left at the desk or giving an address where they could send a letter.

So, by the time we reached Karen's on Thursday evening, it had been a long trip, and I thought maybe Phyllis would have said, "Don't come in tomorrow," or Karen would say, "We always take off a day when we get home from a trip." But it was not to be. Friday was just another working day, although it was the twelfth in a row.

Overtime pay? No such thing.

9

Autumn in New York! It sounded good—and it was. A convention had booked Phyllis to entertain for one night. Really? They were paying for four people to fly cross-country for an hour's appearance and picking up the hotel tab for two nights.

Impressive! Karen was thrilled. Going back to New York for her was like going back to London for me. When Phyllis had played the female lead in the Broadway production of *Hello, Dolly!*, they'd been there for weeks. Karen made plans to get together with friends and show me around.

We arrived late in the afternoon with just half a dozen suitcases this time. Phyllis and Warde had dinner with friends, so Karen and I were free to "go out and play" as Phyllis put it. Karen called her friend Marlene and we went for Chinese food. The lights of New York were everything I expected, as was the frantic pace that everyone embraced. We ate at a cozy Chinese restaurant, obviously one that Karen had patronized many times. Her friends, who owned the restaurant, were happy to see her; she introduced me. We bowed and smiled, and they spoke a language I didn't understand. I wasn't sure exactly what

I was eating, but everything tasted so good, I didn't want to ask. By the time we finished, I was full and tired, and happy that Karen suggested we cab it back to the Plaza.

In the morning I simply had to explore the shops. I suppose New York had a lot of historic sights worth seeing, but I couldn't resist the allure of Fifth Avenue. Karen and I gazed into the windows of the big department stores, and in one of the smaller shops I spotted a pair of boots and fell in love.

"There's no price on them," Karen pointed out. "That's a bad sign."

"Let's just go ask."

Karen trailed me into the posh shop. As I sank into the springy, dark-green carpet, I knew I was way out of my league. The salesman approached with an air of disdain.

"May I help you?" he inquired in a voice that clearly indicated he had little desire to do so. I considered just turning around and leaving, but the place was as empty as a Shea Stadium at Christmas, so I decided I couldn't be infringing too drastically on his time.

"I wanted the price of the boots in the window," I managed in my snootiest voice.

He didn't need to ask which ones; they were the only pair of boots in the window. He smiled glacially and quoted me a price close to the round-trip airfare from L.A. I did not give him the pleasure of seeing me react. I swallowed a gasp, then managed to inquire in my best lady-of-the-manor voice, "And is that each, or for that do I get a pair?"

Before he could reply, Karen and I slid out the door and nearly collapsed laughing on the sidewalk. As I struggled to catch my breath, I sputtered, "I can't believe people would pay so much for something they put on their feet to walk around in the mud."

"So, how about lunch?" she said.

"Isn't there an Automat around here?"

Karen favored me with a look of pure exasperation. We stopped in a little coffee shop and ate sandwiches, then headed back to the hotel and called up to Phyllis's room.

"Warde's gone to visit friends, so it's just us," she said. "You order the car and I'll be right down."

Although she called it a rehearsal, it was really reconnaissance. We needed to find the stage entrance and get the geography of the place.

"Small dressing room," Karen said as she opened the door.

"It's not as close to the stage as I'd like. Check the lights," Phyllis said.

Karen flipped all the switches and lit up the room.

"This is okay. It's hard to put on false eyelashes in the gloom," Phyllis commented as she looked in the mirror.

I figured she'd done it so many times she could probably do it in the dark.

"No lock on the door," Karen said. "I'm not leaving the costume bag here."

I suggested she leave it in the care of the stage manager, but Karen vetoed that. "We'll have to bring it back with us tonight."

The orchestra was rehearsing for the opening-act singer, so I gave them the music for Phyllis's introduction and play-off, both of which were brief. Professional musicians could play it at a glance. The entire outing took less than twenty minutes.

"Back to the hotel," Phyllis told the limo driver; then to us she said, "We'll order from room service."

Neither Karen nor I was hungry, since we'd just had lunch, but Phyllis ordered some soup. We ate it anyway.

Warde had not returned, so Phyllis and I worked on her seemingly never-shrinking stack of correspondence until it was time to leave.

That night I realized another reason Phyllis liked me was that I towered over her. She had a not irrational fear of being hemmed in, and after the night's performance I could see why.

The venue was not a regular theater but a convention facility, so security was minimal. At the end of her performance and before she could get to the dressing room, several people made their way backstage. As soon as they spotted Phyllis, they made a mad dash to say hello. I'm sure they had no intention other than to be friendly, and perhaps they were a little overcome with the thrill of seeing a celebrity, but a dozen excited people bearing down on one can be frightening, especially for a petite woman. People thrust programs at her seeking autographs as other hands reached out to touch her.

"Is this your real hair?" someone shouted as an arm stretched toward her head.

"What a gorgeous costume!" someone else exclaimed as a hand clutched the glittering beads.

"Let me give you a hug!" a large lady screeched as she grabbed Phyllis.

They had backed Phyllis against a wall, and I could sense panic starting as she found herself trapped. I waded into the middle of the group and put a protective arm around her, although ordinarily she didn't like to be touched.

"I'm sorry, we have to leave now," I announced. Putting my other arm out in front of me and stepping on only a few toes, I managed to extract Phyllis and guide her into the dressing room. Karen slammed the door. We all sat quietly for about five minutes, and Phyllis tried to pretend she wasn't rattled. Then came a knock on the door. We froze. When Phyllis nodded, I went to the door and opened it slowly. It was the orchestra leader with our music. I hoped I wasn't too abrupt as I grabbed it out of his hand and slammed the door again.

Once Phyllis had changed out of her costume, I cracked open the door and peeked out. "All clear!" I said and the three of us raced to the waiting limo, Karen dragging the large suitcase and me holding the wig box and the music.

It was well past midnight when we got back to the hotel. We escorted Phyllis to her suite, and Karen got together with her friend Marlene again. I packed and fell into bed.

Warde liked to get to the airport just in the nick of time. His idea of the perfect arrival was to get out of the limousine, be driven in the cart to the gate and step aboard just as the flight attendants readied doors for closing. "I don't like wasting my time sitting around airports," he'd say. We often told Warde a departure time of half an hour sooner than it actually was. The obvious problem with that, of course, was that someday he would catch on. He never did.

That day our flight left at noon and I instructed the limo to pick us up at 10:30. Warde believed the flight took off at 11:30, so he had his bag packed and jacket over his arm at 10:45. He just couldn't ever seem to be on time. I didn't know if he was one of those people who are chronically late or if he wanted to prove that he didn't take orders from anyone.

We got to the airport and walked onto the plane as the flight attendant was preparing to close the door—just the way Warde liked it. Had we followed his schedule and left at 11:00, we would have missed the flight.

10

When we got back to L.A., Warde's older son, Shane, met Phyllis and Warde at the airport with the Rolls Royce. Warde made a big production of getting Phyllis settled in the car. Several heads turned to look.

Karen turned her back and stalked to the baggage area. By that time everything was off the carousel and someone had stacked our collection in a corner. I counted and gave the okay to the skycap. They were all there. As usual, I tipped a generous amount, as Phyllis had instructed. Not only was she generous with skycaps and porters, but she reminded us always to leave tips for the hotel maids.

Because the flight had stopped in St. Louis, it was nearly five o'clock by the time we got back to Phyllis's, and Karen seemed to have recovered from her two nights on the town. "Leave the bags here," she told me as we stacked them inside the front door. "If they know we're here, they'll think of something for us to do." We were gone before anyone realized we'd even been there.

The next morning Maria was all atwitter. "You'll never believe!" she started when I got into the office.

"What won't I believe?" I'd worked there less than two

months and not a single day went by that something didn't surprise me.

"Well," Maria continued with a trace of Castilian accent, "Phyllis's agent, Mr. Moch, called yesterday." Her eyes sparkled. "And guess what?"

"What?"

"You're going to London!"

"London!" For a minute I couldn't catch my breath. "Are you sure?"

"To do the Tom Jones show!" she said, her voice rising.

"London!" I repeated. "When? How many people are they going to pay for?"

"Three," she answered. "Phyllis, Warde, and you."

I was immediately wary. "How do you know the third person will be me?"

"Well, they're paying for two first class and one coach; that's all I know."

I'd thrown a wet blanket on her excitement and her feelings were hurt. She wanted me to be as excited as she, but I wanted it too much to believe it would happen.

"When?"

"The middle of December, right before Christmas."

December wasn't the time of year I would choose to go to London, but what fun it would be to see my friends again. It was exactly a year since I'd left. "I think I'll wait until Phyllis says something before I set my heart on going," I said, but that was a lie. My heart was already set.

Phyllis said nothing about the London trip until the following week. "I know you'd like to go," she mused as we went through her correspondence, "but I think I might take one of the girls" (by which she meant Susie or Stephanie, her teenage daughters).

I tried to mask my disappointment.

"I know you have a lot of friends there," she continued, "and that might be frustrating for you if you had to work and couldn't get together with them."

We couldn't possibly work twenty-four hours a day, I thought.

"Well," she concluded, "we'll have to wait until it gets closer to work something out."

11

For the next five weeks we remained in L.A., Phyllis made occasional appearances on television shows, had fittings for costumes, went to lunch with friends and tried to catch up on correspondence, which generally came in faster than she could handle it.

It was a frustrating time for me. I didn't like working at the house in part because there was no place to get away for lunch. The closest place to eat was a Jack-in-the-Box three miles away. When I brought my lunch from home, the only place to eat was in Phyllis's kitchen. I had thought it would be fun to sit out on the lawn, but a picnic in the front yard didn't appeal to me, and the master bedroom overlooked the side yard. Nobody else seemed to mind, but I found the situation confining and often went for walks at lunchtime, taking Phyllis's little dog, Candy, with me. Once in a while I'd convince Karen to go out for lunch, but otherwise I just stayed in the office and worked through my lunch hour.

As the London trip got closer, I began to get anxious. "I think I'll take Karen to London," Phyllis told me one morning as we were going over the contract for the Tom Jones show. I couldn't imagine any earthly reason why

Phyllis would prefer taking Karen than me, especially when she knew how much Karen hated London.

"After all," she continued as she set down the contract, "she's been there with me before and she knows the way I like things done. I'm afraid you might want to play with your friends when I needed you to do things for me."

Wow, that hurt! Of course if I was going there on business my job took priority. Phyllis couldn't seriously believe I would go off with my friends and neglect the job. It might have had something to do with previous secretaries, but by this time she should have realized she could trust me. I was also piqued that she would imply Karen could do the work better—especially when it came to secretarial things, about which Karen neither knew nor cared. However, it would have been counterproductive to argue.

"Well, of course, you know what you want," I said as casually as I could. "You know I'd love to go, and Karen doesn't like London, so I'm sure if it were up to her, she'd rather not."

Phyllis didn't reply immediately, but when she did, I was certain my approach had been right. I hadn't pushed her into making a decision.

"Well, I'm just not sure what I'm going to do yet."

In this fashion she kept us guessing until almost the day before departure. I never understood her reasoning. Both Susie and Stephanie said they did not want to go, and Karen simply kept her mouth shut on the subject. It seemed as though Phyllis derived a perverse satisfaction out of keeping us dangling. I also wondered how much of it was Warde's doing.

During those weeks, I got to know Ingrid, the college student who worked on the gag file. One day while we were having a coffee break, she mentioned she was going to move to a new apartment. I had already decided it was time for me to get a place of my own since I'd been living with my parents for nearly a year. Ingrid and I fell into the idea of getting a place together and agreed to go apartment shopping right after the first of the year. Although I didn't like the idea of sharing a place, when Karen told me that her apartment had been burgled three times while she was on the road with Phyllis, the thought of having a roommate became more appealing.

My parents and I planned a Christmas party. It looked like it would be the last Christmas I would actually be living at home.

In the meantime, other friends were making Christmas plans, and I realized I couldn't give anyone a definite answer about coming to parties because I didn't know if I'd be in L.A. or in London. On Wednesday afternoon before the Friday departure, Phyllis finally announced her decision. "I know how you like London," she began, "and you probably have a lot of friends at the Embassy." She sat down on the edge of the bed and fixed me with what I'd come to think of as her "earnest look."

This is it. I'm not going.

"I've thought a lot about this. Karen doesn't like London, although she would be the logical one for me to take. After all, there isn't going to be much for a secretary to do at a television taping, but Karen can be helpful with my costumes."

I thought it would be more logical to take a secretary since there would no doubt be phone calls and appointments and perhaps even interviews, but I kept my mouth shut.

"However," she continued, unable to drag it out any longer, "I've decided you'll come with me. Call the travel agent and have them put the third ticket in your name."

I'm going to London! My heart started to pound. I couldn't catch my breath.

Suddenly Phyllis broke into a huge grin. "Are you excited?" she asked.

"Oh, yes! Oh, my gosh! It's like a dream come true!" I squeezed my pen so tight that it bent.

"Well, you know we'll be working all day long, but you'll have evenings free."

"Yes, yes, of course."

"Once we get back from the studio you won't have to hang around."

"Okay. Sure."

Phyllis gave me a big smile. For a moment it seemed almost as if we were a couple of co-eds discussing the upcoming prom.

So many things crowded my mind—I wanted to go back by my old flat in Ashburn Gardens and see what was in the flower boxes, and find out if my charge account at Harrods was still good, and see if my favorite basement bistro was still there, and visit the folk club where I used to hang out Saturday nights. I began to feel dizzy. I couldn't sit still one more minute.

"I have to tell Karen," I said and jumped up. Phyllis just smiled and waved. I was nearly beside myself with excitement. I ran up the stairs, thinking about what clothes to take. It would be cold, of course, perhaps snowy. Rainy for sure. Umbrella! *Where was my umbrella? Did I even have an umbrella?* I laughed out loud as I pushed through the office door. "Karen! Guess what? You're not going to London. Phyllis is taking ME!"

"Thank heaven!" She mopped a hand across her brow as if she'd been sweating.

Maria smiled broadly. "I knew it all along."

"You did? How?"

"I believed it."

Phyllis had read a book called *The Magic of Believing*, which she always said changed her life. Maria had read it as well and adopted the philosophy. The basic premise, as I understood it, was that if you believed something strongly enough, it would come to pass.

"I told you just to believe it," Maria went on with maddening calmness. "You should have just pictured yourself in London, walking along the streets, meeting with your friends. But I did it for you," she concluded in triumph.

I doubted the system worked that way, but she was so pleased, I let it drop.

I had written to a couple of friends and cautiously mentioned I might be seeing them in December. What fun it would be to call and say, "Hey, guess where I am?"

"I have to go home!" I told Karen and Maria. "I have to get packed!"

I took the 405 freeway, pushing my little Volkswagen to the limit. Still, I was in the right-hand lane with traffic zipping by me. When I got home, I burst through the front door.

"I'm going to London!" I yelled.

My dad jumped up from the piano, and Mother came in from the kitchen. We hugged and laughed together.

"Do you want me to take anything to the cleaners?" Mother asked.

"Anything you need to have before you leave?" Dad asked.

"Not a thing. I have to pack." *I'll be in London this weekend!*

12

We left L.A. for London on Friday afternoon at 4:30. The nonstop flight got us there just before noon on Saturday. Colin, the agent from the William Morris Agency, met us, waiting while we went through customs and passport control.

It amused me that even though Phyllis and Warde had gone through customs first (being VIPs, of course), they still had to hang around for me at the back of the pack. At last I emerged from the customs hall and we climbed into the large Rolls Royce the studio had provided. I settled into the front seat next to the chauffeur and ignored the conversation between Phyllis and Colin while we drove into town.

As we neared the city, I began to see familiar landmarks. In no time at all we were through Hammersmith, then Earl's Court and coming to Ashburn Gardens. I strained to catch a glimpse of my old flat, which should have been just visible down the side street from Cromwell Road, but a bus blocked my view as we drove past.

When we reached the Connaught Hotel, I told the limo driver, "Those two bags over there are mine. The rest go upstairs with Phyllis." By the time I got to the suite, Phyllis was going over her schedule with Colin while

Warde busied himself with the red leather "booze bag" he always carried.

"Let's take these bags into the bedroom," I told the porter. It was a large, elegant suite, and we passed through the living room as unobtrusively as possible and into the huge bedroom, which had several wardrobes.

"Those two wig boxes and those two large bags go in this closet here," I told him, pointing to the one by the door. Those were the costumes we'd be taking with us to the studio. "You can set the rest right here."

Thank heaven Phyllis did her own unpacking. I was suddenly tired and anxious to get on to my own hotel. The Tom Jones show only paid for Phyllis's hotel. My room came out of her pocket, so I wouldn't be staying at an expensive hotel like the Connaught. Her attorney/business manager was very careful about how Phyllis spent her money.

"Give me a call when you get up in the morning. Or afternoon," Phyllis said.

With the time change and the long flight, who knew how well any of us would sleep. Phyllis had insisted on arriving a day early so we could get used to the time change.

The Rolls left me and my two suitcases at the Cumberland—a moderately priced Americanized hotel. I unpacked and started calling friends. I desperately wanted to take a nap but knew that if I did, I'd wake up at midnight and would feel even worse the next day. Instead, I called Richard, an old flame, and made a date for dinner. Since there were still a couple of hours until dark, I went outside. I bundled up in my warm Spanish cape and pushed through the massive revolving door. The cold, sharp air took my breath away. Just what I needed.

"Evening, miss," the doorman said. "Can I get you a taxi?"

"No, thanks, I want to walk."

The shops all closed at noon on Saturday, but that was okay. Instead I strolled through Hyde Park and thought about the two years I'd spent working at the Embassy. I'd loved my years as a secretary in the Administrative Section. The fact that my boss had the final okay on the guest list for a host of Embassy-related parties worked out well. My name had mysteriously made its way onto the invitation list for the Diplomatic Tea at Buckingham Palace, so I'd taken tea with Her Majesty. I and 999 other people. I'd also been invited to the opening day of the races at Royal Ascot in the Queen's Pavilion. It was a private, invitation-only area for 3,000 of Her Majesty's closest friends.

My social life had worked out pretty well, too, I reflected as I walked through Hyde Park. I'd started dating one of the Marine Guards soon after I arrived in London. After he returned to the States, I'd gone out with a variety of nice Englishmen—oh, yes, I'd had a blast in London.

As I walked through Hyde Park, I remembered one particularly lovely summer afternoon when I'd been so enthralled with the joy of being in this storied place that I'd taken off my shoes and walked barefoot through the soft, green grass. As I reveled in the sheer beauty of it all, a man called out to me: "Hey, lady, that grass is full of dog shit." *Oh, thank you so much.* Remembering that incident, I laughed out loud.

On the other side of Hyde Park, I caught the Number 12 bus on Knightsbridge and rode it to Cromwell Road, past Harrods, which I planned to visit later. It was only two blocks to Ashburn Gardens, and there it was—my old home. Five Ashburn Gardens was a lovely four-story building with a black door and white pillars, just like all the other buildings that surrounded the little garden. The caretaker, Mrs. Harris, lived in the basement flat; I had lived on the first floor, which in the U.S. would be the second floor because what we called the first floor, they called the ground floor. It had taken me a while to get used to that. My window boxes sat empty and seeing them left me sad. Perhaps the people living there just couldn't afford to buy plants. Or maybe they were waiting for spring. *Yeah, I'll bet that's it.*

I took a walk around the gardens until I started to get chilly. *Time to get inside!* I flagged a taxi to take me back to the hotel. By the time Richard picked me up for dinner, I'd luxuriated in a hot bubble bath and got my second wind. Even so, I told him I wanted to make it an early evening.

I had met Richard shortly before my tour at the Embassy concluded. He was one of several Englishmen I'd dated. I had no serious attachment with any of them, and in a couple of cases, I wondered if they saw me as something of a novelty: a cute American girl from the U.S. Embassy. Richard and I corresponded after I left, and he was one of the few people who knew that I might be visiting. Over dinner I told him about my new life in show business and he laughed at some of the tales.

"Why so many suitcases, especially an office bag and a kitchen bag?"

"Phyllis is very particular about everything, especially her costumes and props, and, believe it or not, she likes to cook for us occasionally."

As our delightful and delicious evening drew to a close, Richard walked me back to the hotel, where he left me in the lobby with a hug. I felt happy to have spent a lovely time with him and, with a full tummy, I took the elevator to my room. I barely managed to put on my nightgown before I fell asleep.

Surprisingly, I did not sleep late the next day. When I opened my eyes, my travel alarm said 9:30 A.M. London time, and I had to stop myself from figuring the time difference to California. It was a silly thing to do and made no difference whatsoever. It being Sunday morning, I thought about attending the morning church service at the Guards Chapel. I'd loved going there while I was with the Embassy. Regimental flags hung from the ceiling and the service was traditional, the liturgy soothingly repetitive, and it always ended with *God Save the Queen* and the Navy hymn, *Eternal Father, Strong to Save.* I don't think I learned much about God or the Bible, but it was so incredibly English and conventional that no matter how hectic the week had been, I left comforted with the knowledge that in spite of famine, wars, and plagues, the world had gone on for centuries and would likely continue for many more. It put my little problems in perspective.

But my friend Kay, whom I'd called after checking in, had left a message at the front desk while I was out with Richard: "Brunch tomorrow. My place. Noon."

It was too early for Phyllis to be up, but I called anyway. Sure enough, the operator at the Connaught told me they had a "do not disturb" on their phone. (I hadn't even known it was possible to do that until I'd begun traveling with Phyllis.)

Brunch at Kay's apartment turned into a reunion. Kay had invited several friends I'd worked with. My British friends didn't know much about Phyllis Diller because her shows had not been on the telly there. But still they were pleased that I had such a great job and got to travel. Or at least I hoped I would do more traveling. Besides the trip to London, I'd only been to Pittsburgh and New York.

While at Kay's, I called Phyllis's suite. Three o'clock and they had just finished breakfast.

"Are you having fun?" Phyllis asked after I told her where I was.

"Absolutely!"

"Well, I don't think there's anything I'm going to need today. We're going out with Colin for dinner and we leave at seven in the morning for the studio."

I heard Warde say something in the background.

"Hold on," Phyllis said as she put her hand over the mouthpiece. I could hear a muffled conversation, then Phyllis came back on the line.

"Warde wants to know if you're sure you got all the bags off the plane. He seems to be missing something."

My heart sank. I could imagine all the fuss and furor I would have to go through to retrieve a missing piece of luggage. On Sunday, no less.

Why the hell hadn't he noticed it yesterday?

I thought back, remembering which bags we had brought with us. I couldn't imagine I'd overlooked one. I was sure I had counted them all at least half a dozen times. I'd counted them at the airport as they came off the carousel, again after we'd gone through customs, and also when the porter stashed them in the boot of the car. At the hotel, I made certain that all the bags were out of the car, I counted again after the porter brought them inside, and I watched to be sure that all the bags were taken to the suite.

"No, I'm sure we've got them all," I replied. "Which one does he think is lost?"

"Which bag, Warde?" I heard Phyllis ask. There was more conversation between them while in my mind I counted the bags once again. There was no way one had gone astray.

"He doesn't know which bag it was," she said, "but he's sure he brought his suede jacket, and he can't find it."

"Have you checked all the wardrobes?" I vaguely remembered the porter opening closet doors after he brought up the bags.

Phyllis called out to Warde. "Is it in one of the wardrobes?"

I heard only silence for nearly a minute, then Phyllis came back on the line. "We've found it," she said. "It was in the closet behind the coats."

What a relief! I had visions of my entire afternoon being spent trying to track down a nonexistent bag at the airport.

"Well, I guess that's it," Phyllis concluded. "Remember, the car's going to pick us all up here at seven tomorrow." I wondered why Colin, or whoever had made the arrangements with the car, hadn't had the forethought to ask them to stop by the Cumberland at 6:55 and get me first, but that was a minor inconvenience compared to having the rest of the day to myself.

Kay served mimosas—champagne with orange juice—and we all chatted a long while. Some of my friends left, and after a bit someone suggested the four of us who remained go to a bistro, which was halfway between Kay's flat and my hotel. It would be an easy walk.

The bistro specialized in French country food and although I thought I'd never eat again after the spread Kay laid out, I put away the better part of a *coq au vin*. We had talked and laughed for longer than I realized because when I glanced outside, it was fully dark. *How did it get so late so fast?*

"Hey," I said, "tomorrow's a working day for all of us. It's been great seeing you, but I'm going to head back to the hotel."

There were hugs all around and I promised to drop by the Embassy before I left London.

The next morning the alarm went off at 5:30. *An unearthly hour to get out of bed.* It was still dark when I went downstairs. I stamped my feet in the cold as the doorman whistled up a taxi.

At the Connaught, I debated about going up to the room or ringing from the lobby. The simultaneous arrivals of the elevator and the Rolls solved my dilemma. Phyllis stepped out of the elevator, followed by Warde and a porter carrying the two large costume suitcases and a wig box. The porter stowed the bags in the car, and, with a mumbled greeting, Phyllis and Warde crawled into the back seat. I again slid up front with the driver for the hour-long ride.

At the studio I stepped out of the luxurious Rolls into the still dark and cold English climate and recalled the downside to life in the British Isles. I wrapped my cape around me and wiggled my toes in my knee-high boots. As usual, Phyllis was bundled in an ankle-length fur coat. "It's the only thing that really keeps me warm," she always said. She wore her white mink along with her usual white shirt, slacks, and shoes, and she had pulled a white hood over her head. In the morning twilight she looked like a small, furry ghost scampering into the studio.

Inside, everything was warm and bright. People walked about and talked as if it weren't the middle of the night for those of us from California. Colin appeared and guided us to the dressing room, introducing Phyllis to everyone along the way.

Right off, Phyllis and Warde attended a production meeting with Colin. I stayed in the dressing room, hanging up costumes and arranging the dressing table in my best imitation of Karen's style. The door opened an hour later.

"Why don't you go downstairs and watch?" Phyllis suggested. "My monologue is taping after lunch. I don't need you right now."

Murmuring a silent prayer of thanks, I headed for the stairs, delighted to be out of the close quarters with the three of them.

I picked up a production schedule lying on a table downstairs and saw that in addition to her stand-up monologue, Phyllis was scheduled to perform skits with Tom Jones on Tuesday and Wednesday, and a closing number on Thursday with Tom Jones and his other guest star, Tony Bennett. An audience began filing in and I joined them, taking a seat on the end of a row.

It seemed to take forever to tape even a small segment. Setting up for Phyllis's part that afternoon was tedious. First they had to get light readings off the costume and jewelry (the rhinestone-covered dog collar that Phyllis had on gave the lighting man fits), then there were camera angles and sound levels. They had to allow for laughter from the audience and endless discussions took place between the director and the production people concerning heaven only knows what.

Finally, after starting and stopping several times, they got the entire five-minute monologue taped. The audience laughed far more than I had expected and at the end burst into applause. Phyllis beamed with pleasure.

My friends might be in for a surprise.

"Okay, that's a wrap!" the director called. "Miss Diller, we'll see you tomorrow."

Back we went to the dressing room, and once assured that it would be locked up, Phyllis agreed to leave everything as is. She changed and the three of us piled into the Rolls for the drive back into town.

The sun had not quite set, and Warde came alive, looking forward to the evening and their get-together with friends. Phyllis was a little less enthusiastic and no wonder—she'd been working all day. I was good and tired. I slurped some soup in the hotel restaurant and headed upstairs to bed. *No partying for me tonight!*

The next morning we didn't have to leave so early since once again Phyllis wasn't taping until after lunch. I went to the American Embassy and met the secretary who had taken my job. I also saw a lot of my old friends and poked my head into Kay's office.

"Just heading out," I told her. "We're leaving at noon for the studio."

"Can I ask you a favor?" she said as she walked me to the elevator.

"Sure."

"My sister is the biggest Tom Jones fan in the world, and she would be thrilled beyond words to have his autograph. Do you think you could?"

"Well, um, sure. I guess. I haven't even met him yet, but if I get a chance, I'll ask."

"Don't go out of your way, but if it works out, you know she would love it."

I thought about Kay's request as I headed for the Connaught. I didn't know anything about Tom Jones and wasn't sure he was the kind of person one could approach for an autograph.

At the hotel, the Rolls waited out front, and I called Phyllis from the lobby.

Warde answered. "She's on her way down."

"Are you coming, too?" I asked.

"Not today."

I couldn't say I blamed him since there was nothing for him to do. We drove out in silence as Phyllis studied her script. One of her pet peeves was people who didn't know their lines. About thirty minutes into the drive, I saw a farm with a lot of horses. They looked old. A sign read "Horse Haven."

"What's that?" I asked the driver.

"It's a home for retired horses," he said. "Old working horses like they use to pull carts. When they get too broken down to work, they used to send them to the glue factory." He chuckled. "Now they send 'em here."

Phyllis looked up. She loved animals. "How long do they stay here?" she asked as we drove by another pasture.

"Rest of their lives, ma'am. Rest of their lives, bless 'em."

It was so typically English. The old, useless animals who'd spent a lifetime pulling a cart through the city streets from before dawn till long past dark were enjoying the rest of their days on a farm where the grass was always green and the stalls were warm and dry. I wondered if their owners had such a happy retirement.

In another few minutes, we pulled up to the studio gate. The driver pointed out a large house trailer. "That's Tom Jones's dressing room."

Both Phyllis and I stared at it as if it being Tom Jones's dressing room would somehow make it different from other house trailers.

"It's said to move about a foot a day," he continued.

Phyllis and I looked at each other, then back at the trailer.

"It does?" she replied.

"Yeah," the driver said. "Like this." And with his hand held out flat, he made a back-and-forth motion as though he were sanding a floor.

I still didn't get it. I looked back at Phyllis and she whispered, "Screwing."

Oh!

The driver broke out in a huge laugh and Phyllis did, too.

Inside, Phyllis went right to makeup. She normally did her own, but television makeup is different, not just because of the close-ups but because of the quality of lighting. Phyllis still put on her own false eyelashes, however.

"The green dress," Phyllis told me as she sat at the dressing table. She did the eyelashes, stepped into the dress, and pulled on the fright wig.

"Makeup," a lady said from the doorway. "Do you need a touch-up?"

Phyllis checked the mirror. "No, I'm okay. Thank you."

She put on the boots and dog collar, and we headed downstairs for her skit with Tom Jones.

"Careful he doesn't latch on to you," she warned me as we descended the stairs. "He has quite an eye for the ladies." Then she held her hand flat, making the same back-and-forth motion as the chauffeur and laughed.

I wondered if Tom Jones would actually hit on me. *What would I do? Would I tell Phyllis? Would I spend the next three days hiding out in the dressing room? Surely he had all the women he needed.* I'd heard stories of women throwing their underwear onto the stage. When we reached the set, Tom Jones was already there chatting with the crew. Colin appeared and made introductions. I tried to hide behind Phyllis, but that didn't work.

The famous singer shook my hand and smiled. "Welcome to my show."

When he glanced away, Phyllis nudged me and winked. I blushed all the way to my toes.

What impressed me most was that he was having a great time and his attitude affected everyone. It seemed more like fun than work. No audience appeared that day, so I settled in a front-row seat, clutching the Gucci note pad I always carried. One of Phyllis's favorite expressions was, "Robin, make a note of that."

The taping went smoothly and quickly. The longest pauses were for resetting the cameras. It didn't go as fast as I'd thought, however, because when we left the studio, unlike the day before, the sun had already set, and we drove back to the hotel in the dark.

At the Connaught, Phyllis scrambled out of the Rolls. "Warde and I are having dinner with friends tonight," she said. "Be here tomorrow at nine. Have a good night." She smiled and went inside. It had been a good day.

I'd enjoyed the taping. Things there seemed a bit more relaxed than the tapings I'd been to in L.A. Perhaps it was because of Tom Jones, or just that there seemed far fewer people on the set. I smiled as I went into the restaurant, where I ordered a dinner of fish and chips. On the one hand, I felt like I should be making the most of the brief time I had in London, but on the other hand, I had already seen and done a lot.

I knew we would have all day free on Friday and Saturday, so I could do my shopping then. I'd already made plans for Friday night to get together with an American friend, Peggy, who lived in London. Saturday night I was going back to The Troubadour, the folk club near my flat that I'd often visited when I lived there. *This week is working out very well indeed.*

On day three, Phyllis had two more skits. I'd awakened incredibly refreshed and felt energized and ready to take on the world. I didn't have a lot to do, and in between helping her with her costumes, I sat on the edge of the set with some of the makeup ladies. We had fallen into conversation between takes and every one of them told me how much they loved working on the show.

"Tom is such a sweetheart," one of the girls said, and the others all nodded or murmured their agreement.

"He's such a kind person, not stuck-up at all," one added. "He's sort of like the boy next door."

"Wouldn't I like to have someone like that living next door to me!" another of the girls hooted.

The audience, which had returned, seemed to agree as well. The people again laughed and loudly applauded each scene. After Phyllis finished taping her first bit with Tom, she headed back to the dressing room with Warde, who had joined her that day.

"You don't need to come up," Phyllis told me. "Why

don't you stay and watch the taping awhile. I've got a break until they finish this next scene."

Tom and Tony Bennett had a number where they played pool. The crew was just getting out a billiards table, so I settled back down with the makeup girls as Tom Jones strolled across the set. He chatted with several of the production people, then wandered over to the audience.

"How are you today?" he asked the group.

They all answered pleasantly, although somewhat subdued. They probably hadn't been expecting anything quite that up close and personal.

"Has anyone got any questions about the show?"

One or two people asked timid questions, then the director yelled, "Places please, everybody."

With a wave of his hand, Tom Jones strolled to his mark and the cameras began to roll. Between takes, Tom stood around chatting with whoever happened to be there, and several more times stopped to talk to the audience. In the scene they played pool, drank from brandy snifters, and smoked big cigars. They also sang, of course. They'd barely started when the director shouted for the cameras to stop.

"Okay, here's the deal," he said. "You can't be playing pool while you're singing. I'm getting too much interference from the clicking of the balls."

"It doesn't matter," Tom shot back. "I can't ever hit the balls anyway."

Everyone laughed. They discussed it for a moment. "How about this," the director finally offered. "We'll shoot you singing and walking around the pool table, and you can set up like you're going to hit the balls, but then we'll cut away. We'll take some scenes later where you're actually playing pool and intercut them."

"Sounds good to me," somebody said, and everyone

else agreed. They taped a bit more, then took a break to reset the cameras. While they were doing that, Tom Jones came over to the area where we were sitting. He greeted the girls all by name.

No wonder they like working here. He really does act like the boy next door.

He flopped down into a chair and chatted with us until the director announced they were ready to resume shooting. Far from being thunderstruck or shy, the girls treated the star as one of their own, and I could see why everyone on the show seemed so comfortable with each other.

"We're going to have to do something about those cigars," the script girl noted. She had to see that they maintained continuity.

"This is only an eight-minute scene, but you've already gone through an entire cigar. That's going to look funny."

The prop man produced new cigars, and they were cut down to the size they had been when they interrupted taping.

Tom walked back to where we were sitting and dropped his cigar butt into the ashtray on a nearby table before returning to the set. In all that time, I had not seen anything to suggest he'd be making his trailer move a foot a day, as the chauffeur had told us. He'd been nothing but a gentleman. While he'd chatted with the girls, he was neither flirtatious nor suggestive. I wondered how much of that rumor was publicity—or perhaps he saved his "wanderings" for people he didn't work with and see every day.

I waited until they had resumed shooting, then at the first break asked the girls as casually as I could, "Does anyone want that?"

"Want what?" one of them asked.

I motioned to the cigar butt.

They looked at me as if I'd lost my mind.

"It's not for me," I assured them, as I extracted a wad of tissues from my purse. "It's for the sister of a friend of mine."

They all smiled knowingly, and I felt myself blush as I picked up the smelly thing. It seemed a wonderful souvenir. *Tom Jones actually smoked this very cigar!* I could hardly wait to see Kay the next day to give it to her.

Once the segment ended and they prepared for Phyllis's skit, I hurried to the dressing room. I found a little plastic bag to wrap the cigar in. (Even through the plastic, it smelled up my purse so horribly that I was afraid the purse would be ruined for good. I did, actually, get rid of the purse after we got back to the U.S. That cigar smell just would not go away.) Warde came in while Phyllis was fluffing up her fright wig.

"That guy doesn't know what he's doing," he announced as he pushed through the door.

"What guy, Warde?" Phyllis asked without looking up.

"Tom Jones!"

I hadn't seen Warde on the set, but obviously he'd stayed to watch some of the scenes being taped. I busied myself with folding more tissues to put in my purse. Phyllis had a deviated septum, which caused her nose to drip frequently, and Karen and I always carried tissues for her.

"What's he doing?" Phyllis asked as she slipped the wig on.

"Well, he stands around the set just talking to everyone. He even goes over to the audience and talks to them!" His voice dripped scorn. "That's not the way to be a star!"

"Well, what's he supposed to do between takes?" Phyllis asked. "He has to go somewhere."

"That's just it! You don't stand around and let the audience look at you. You just give them a little bit here and a little bit there. He should go back to his dressing room between takes." Warde postured outrageously, strutting up and down, puffing out his chest and tossing his head to demonstrate how he would treat an audience. "He doesn't know what he's doing."

Phyllis looked at him for a moment, then said, "I'm going downstairs. Are you coming?"

As I trailed after them, I couldn't help thinking, *Well, Mr. Donovan, I guess that's why you're such a big star and he's a nobody.*

13

The show finished up Thursday evening, and we still had Friday and Saturday before we would leave London. In the Rolls, Phyllis relaxed. Although she liked to work, I knew she was happy to have the show finished.

"I'm going to do some Christmas shopping," I told her.

"Where do you shop?"

"Harrods sometimes, but I love Marks and Spencer. They have their own brand and it's not expensive."

"Do they have pantyhose? I'm wearing my last pair."

"Marks and Spencer has everything."

"Take me with you," she said.

So it happened that Phyllis Diller went to a store usually frequented by working-class folk. I'd been apprehensive, but if anyone noticed a lady wearing an ankle-length mink coat and a white wool hood, they probably marked her down as an eccentric American and let it go at that.

"Look at these sweaters!" she said. "Wouldn't they be perfect for Stephanie and Susie?" She dropped them into the basket I was holding. In the next aisle, she scooped up an armload of blouses. "I hope we're going to have room to pack all this."

You and me both.

She filled a basket with the pantyhose and delighted in finding men's socks. She grabbed a half dozen pairs in each color for the boys. When Phyllis decided to do something, she did it in a big way.

Some of the things I had planned to buy were going to take up a lot of room, too, such as Bromley bath oil and boxes of scented soap. I hoped I could cram everything into my large Pullman and had already decided I could snug some of the smaller things into the office bag. I had counted on her leaving autographed copies of her books for a lot of people and that would make room. I hoped that same thought hadn't occurred to Phyllis.

Saturday afternoon I took the cigar to Kay. "You're not going to believe this," I said. "This is a cigar that Tom Jones actually smoked himself!"

She looked at the plastic bag that I held out to her. "It smells," she said.

"Yeah. It's a cigar. It's for your sister."

"Oh-kay."

"She'll love it! I even found out the episode number so she can be sure to watch. She'll have to check the *TV Guide* to see when it's on in her city. It's much better than an autograph. Autographs get lost or torn. Nobody else in the world has a cigar that Tom Jones actually smoked."

"Uh-huh." Kay seemed less than enthusiastic about my stinky offering, but she took it.

"Really. She's going to love it."

Kay held it gingerly and I wondered if she'd dropped it down the trash chute as soon as I left.

By the time of our departure, I was ready to leave London. Never thought that would be possible. I'd seen all of my friends and partied late and early. I'd done my

Christmas shopping, gone back to Harrods, and even had time for a few sentimental journeys.

It took some creative packing, but I managed to get everything stuffed into those two suitcases. Thank goodness Phyllis hadn't said anything to me about putting her purchases in my office bag. Apparently she'd figured out a way to get them all in her bags. Or Warde's.

We left London on Sunday afternoon and, after a ten-hour flight, arrived in L.A. the same afternoon, only two hours later by the clock. My dad met me at the airport, and Phyllis's son, Perry, came to get her and Warde. As she crawled into the Rolls, Phyllis turned and called to me, "Don't come in tomorrow."

Thank heaven!

14

Christmas came and went with all the attendant parties and get-togethers. Everyone loved the presents I brought from London, and my brother called from Houston to say the soap I'd sent him "smelled delicious." It's just not a thing guys would buy for themselves, I knew—sandalwood soap.

Ingrid called me New Year's Day. "Happy New Year! Are you ready to start looking for an apartment?"

"Today?"

"Sure. Why not?"

I couldn't think of any reason not to. Over the next several days we spent every spare moment looking at likely places. Ingrid had more free time than I did, and I was thrilled when she found a place on Beverly Glen Boulevard, just south of San Vicente.

"It's only a few miles from Phyllis's," she told me over the phone.

She gave me the address and I met her there. "What a find! This will drastically cut down my commute from the San Fernando Valley," I said.

The building sprawled nearly half a block on the side of a hill. It was old, but it featured multilevel courtyards with wrought-iron benches shaded by banana and palm trees. Best of all, it had a swimming pool in the center courtyard. It was right at the top or our price range, but oh so worth it!

I used the Christmas bonus from Phyllis to buy a mattress for my brass bed. I'd gotten the bed in England when I worked at the Embassy. That and a glass-topped coffee table from South Africa were the only furniture I owned.

"I've got a couch and a couple of easy chairs," Ingrid said as we surveyed the place. It would be sparse, but what the heck. Who needed furniture?

We'd just moved in when it came time for Phyllis's next trip—two weeks at the Riviera Hotel in Las Vegas.

"You're going to love working Las Vegas," Karen said. "It's a piece of cake. No interviews, no promotions, nothing like that. People always come to see the shows on the Strip. There is one thing—make sure our rooms are as far from hers as possible. Out of sight, out of mind."

When I talked to the agent at William Morris, I felt odd bringing up the subject of hotel rooms, so I didn't. It turned out that our rooms were on a different floor from Phyllis's because the suites for the stars and big gamblers were on the top floor. Karen and I were considerably below that.

Karen was right; everything about Las Vegas was easy. The flight took forty-five minutes. When we landed, the airline PSR took Phyllis and Warde out a side gate directly from the plane to the waiting limousine. Las Vegas was used to celebrities.

When we got to the hotel, Karen and I separated the bags.

"I'll take Phyllis's up to the suite," she said. "You get us organized."

I stopped at the front desk to check us in and get our keys. The manager had already given Phyllis and Warde their keys, but Phyllis wanted Karen or me to have a key to their room as well. Checking us all in was basically a formality and took only a few minutes.

While I was at the desk, I made the arrangements for the phone calls as Karen had instructed: all of Phyllis's calls would come to me. If I was not in my room, then Phyllis would be paged, but I would answer the page. The hotel policy was to have its entertainers paged by name whenever possible for the publicity and to let people know they were there. If no one answered the page, then the messages would be put in my box. (Those were the days before voice mail on hotel phones.) In the evenings, the calls would be put through to the dressing room backstage. There were only a few people whose calls went directly to Phyllis: her children, her agent, her publicist, and her attorney. Once that was settled, I followed the bellman up to our rooms. I had just stepped inside the door when the phone rang. It was Phyllis.

"Are you all settled in?" she asked—her polite way of saying she was ready to work. I would have to unpack later.

Before I left my room, I opened the office bag and took out two dozen scratch pads and a dozen sharpened pencils. I also took four dozen pens—a dozen each of black, blue, red, and green. Phyllis wanted pens and scratch pads always within reach. She expected a note pad and a pen by every phone.

"Nothing is more irritating," she told me, "than calling someone and have them say, 'Wait a minute while I get something to write on,' unless it's having that person call you and then ask you to wait."

As soon as I got into the suite I started setting out the pads, pencils, and one pen of each color on every flat surface. The pens were color-coded: black for phone messages, blue for notes relating to work, red to file in her "gag file," and green for an idea she wanted to keep or expand. She had dozens of these notes in her room, both on the road and at home. How she managed to keep track of everything was a mystery to me. I was not entirely sure that she always did.

While I did that, Warde called their favorite restaurant for dinner reservations between shows.

"Not on opening night," Phyllis said when she heard him making plans for that evening, and Warde hastily changed the reservation.

Phyllis didn't actually want to work; she just wanted to be sure everything was in place. I checked the cards on the dozens of red roses that filled the room. They were from her agent, publicist, and a couple of friends. Later, I would write thank-you notes for her to sign. I didn't sign them because Phyllis would want to read what I'd written and, besides that, she never minded signing personal correspondence. "That's what makes it personal," she told me.

Rehearsal was at 5:00, and Phyllis told me to come back to the suite at a quarter to. That just gave me time to do my own unpacking. Before I left to go back upstairs, I called Karen's room but got no answer.

As I arrived at the suite, Phyllis called out, "Warde, are you coming?"

"Be there in a minute, Ada," he answered.

Ada was Warde's pet name for her. It was her middle name and as far as I knew, he was the only one who called her that.

Phyllis glanced at me as we waited for Warde. "I'm going to show you the back way to the dressing room." It turned out to be through the kitchen, which rather than being filled with wonderful odors of exotic food, smelled like wet garbage and cauliflower. Yuck!

Karen had finished laying out the accessories by the time we walked in. Dog collars, false eyelashes, and cigarette holders spread across white towels to the left of the mirror. On the right were the jars of makeup, and in the middle a clock that looked like a very large pocket watch. Phyllis opened the top drawer and I could see her gloves, all arranged in pairs by color.

Over the speaker in the dressing room, we could hear John Davidson, Phyllis's opening act, rehearsing. (After the fiasco at the Holiday House in Pittsburgh, she never let Warde be her opening act again.)

Phyllis didn't have much to rehearse. In fact, she didn't even have to be there, but being a professional, she was. Warde passed out the music to the orchestra and explained which was her play-on and play-off music. He did her introduction from backstage, then the band played some snappy music as she dashed out.

Phyllis talked briefly to the light man about the overhead banks of lights. "All warm colors," she told him. The mix of yellow, red, and pink were flattering to the skin. (One time Warde insisted that blue was a warm color, but nobody paid attention.) The lights were set and the only thing about them that changed was the "travel spot," which followed her. Once the curtain came down behind her, she would be in the spotlight all by herself for forty minutes. At the end, the band would play her exit music and keep it up long enough for her to take a bow, then she'd dash offstage, and that would be it. While she was actually performing, one of the stagehands would have to "page" the microphone cord, keeping it fairly taut so she wouldn't trip on it as she pranced across the stage (in the days before wireless mikes).

As soon as rehearsal was finished, Warde and Phyllis went through the kitchen and back to the suite. Karen was itching to play the slots, so she dragged me into the casino. That was the first time in my adult life I had been to Las Vegas, and I was excited by the whole atmosphere.

I had been to the Riviera many years before when we had taken a family trip to Chicago. We had stopped in Las Vegas long enough to see an actual casino. My parents still had a picture of me standing by the pool at this very hotel.

As Karen flagged down a change girl and got a roll of quarters, I strolled around, taking in the action; it was early enough that the casino wasn't packed, and I could easily stand and watch over the shoulders of people at the blackjack tables, and watch the fast and furious betting at the craps tables. What really interested me, though, was roulette. It reminded me of an elegant weekend I'd spent in Swaziland when I was in the Foreign Service. I decided that if I did any gambling at all, it would be roulette.

Phyllis did two shows a night and after the second show, which ended at one-thirty in the morning, I went with Karen to gamble. I watched her feed quarters into a slot machine for a few minutes, then sidled up to the rou_lette table. A sheik was there—an honest-to-goodness Arabian sheik. He wore a flowing robe from which he pulled a series of hundred-dollar bills. I was so fascinated that I changed a ten-dollar bill into chips just so I could stand next to him and watch. I bet a dollar a spin and he bet $100 a spin. I couldn't tell if he had a system, but whatever he was doing, it wasn't working. I'd never seen anyone lose money so consistently. I'd started with $10 and left with $12. *Whoopee*. I walked away a winner! At least until the following night.

The casino had lovely chandeliers, and Phyllis told me that the Riviera and the Desert Inn were the two casinos that catered to the "high rollers."

As I walked around enjoying the action, I couldn't help thinking, *I'm Phyllis Diller's personal secretary. I'm part of what makes all this happen.* It was like having a delicious secret.

On the Road With Phyllis Diller

The shows went perfectly and the absolute professionalism impressed me. Orchestra members wore tuxedos or black cocktail dresses (depending on their sex, of course), and the stagehands, who were also dressed in black, worked quickly and quietly.

"Why are they all wearing black?" I asked Karen. "Is it like a uniform?"

"Because if they ever get in the audience sight line they won't be obvious." Once she'd said it, of course, it made sense.

I didn't have a thing to do, so the stage manager, Bob, let me sit in his office while Phyllis performed. He impressed me by always being one jump ahead of whatever was going on. No wonder Karen liked to work in Las Vegas—it was virtually a holiday. Besides that, Bob was a hunk and a nice guy, too.

On the second day, the phone rang in my room and a lady asked for Phyllis.

"She isn't in at the moment. This is her secretary, may I help?" (My standard response.)

"Would you ask her to give me a call," the lady replied. "My name is Totie Fields." I jotted it down and repeated the number she gave me.

"Will she know who you are, or can I tell her what this is in reference to?" I asked. I'd learned my lesson from the milk commercial. I wasn't taking any incomplete messages to Phyllis.

There was a slight pause. "I'm a friend of Phyllis's" came the polite reply.

"I'll give her the message as soon as she returns."

When I went up to the suite later that afternoon and handed over the note, I apologized for the lack of details. "I couldn't find out what she wanted," I said, "but she said you know her."

Phyllis looked at me and started to laugh. That laugh is

great onstage but rather overpowering in a closed space. Finally she caught her breath and reached for the *What's On* entertainment guide. She thumbed through it until she came to a full-page ad for the International Hotel. It read in half-inch letters, "The Las Vegas International Hotel is proud to present . . ." And in inch-high letters, "TOTIE FIELDS!"

"Oh," I said feebly. By the time I had absorbed the fact that it must've been the same Totie Fields, Phyllis had her on the phone.

"Totie! It's good to hear from you." Pause. "I got your message." Laugh. "New secretary. Her name is Robin." Pause. "No, no. It's just that I've trained her to think I'm the only comedienne in the world!"

Prolonged boisterous laughter from both ends of the phone.

Well, live and learn.

Totie asked Phyllis and Warde to dinner in her new house.

"What can I bring?" Phyllis asked. "Really? You don't even have furniture?"

As soon as she hung up the phone, Phyllis began putting on her "uniform."

"Call Karen," she said, "and get the car. Come on, Warde, we're going shopping. Totie just moved into a new house. She told me the only thing I need to bring is something to sit on. We need to find some secondhand shops."

The hotel provided Phyllis with a car. Karen got to drive. I sat up front.

It wasn't long before we were crawling along Main Street past Al's Used Furniture, Bi-Rite Furniture, and the A-Z Mart, all of which had merchandise displayed on the sidewalk in front. Phyllis decided the last one looked promising and Karen maneuvered the Lincoln Continental into a space relatively near the curb. Phyllis and Warde hopped out and I followed behind like a lady-in-waiting, carrying the money. Karen opted to stay with the car. She had been on those shopping sprees before.

After they looked through the store, Phyllis pulled me aside.

"Find out how much that chair is," she whispered rather loudly as she pointed. "If they know it's for me, they'll jack up the price."

I figured that horse was already out of the barn, but I did as instructed.

"It's only twenty-five dollars," the man said, trying hard not to look at Phyllis and Warde as they tried equally hard to be inconspicuous.

Twenty-five dollars didn't seem very "only" for an obviously used straight-back chair, no matter who was buying it.

While that was going on, Phyllis wandered through the rest of the shop and found a lamp that was "perfect" (for what I wasn't sure) and a large picture of Jesus in a solid-looking frame. She pointed out the objects of her desire, and I paid for them as she returned to the car. Warde actually made himself useful by carrying the lamp and helping to get the chair stowed. We drove sedately back to the hotel with the rather large chair protruding from the trunk.

"Have the bellmen bring everything up to the suite," Phyllis instructed as she and Warde alighted. If I felt somewhat odd following a parade of three bellmen, one carrying a chair, one a lamp, and the other a nearly life-size portrait of Jesus, I felt even odder that evening as I followed another bellman through the casino carrying the chair, now festooned with bright red ribbons that Phyllis had taken off the fruit baskets in her suite.

The bellman had been reluctant to take the chair from the room, insinuating that I must be stealing hotel property. There had been a change of shifts since our shopping expedition, so he'd not seen the earlier procession. I managed to convince him, however, that the Riviera Hotel certainly wouldn't furnish its suites with obviously secondhand furniture. He checked it carefully before he agreed to take it down to the car.

Of all the bellmen in the hotel, that one in particular managed to convey his disapproval of Phyllis, me, entertainment, and gambling in general, all without saying a word. Unfortunately, he also showed up two weeks later when we called for help in packing. Neither the lamp nor the large picture would fit in a suitcase. When he arrived and I had explained we needed to have them packed for shipping, he scrutinized both objects, fixed me with a baleful stare, then looked once more at the picture.

"That is a beautiful picture of our Lord," he intoned in an undertaker's voice.

"Yes. Yes, it is." I hoped he hadn't noticed, but knew he had, that Phyllis had "autographed" the picture for her publicist. In a bold, black scrawl she had written: "To Frank Lieberman, who made me what I am today."

That happened two weeks later, though. That night all I cared about was getting the damned chair delivered and trying not to look as foolish as I felt trailing the surly bellman past all the elegantly gowned ladies and besuited gentlemen. And Phyllis had made it worse by giving me specific instructions to see to it personally that the chair was delivered to Totie Fields' dressing room.

"Don't just leave it with a bellman," she told me. "I want you to make sure it gets where it's going. If you leave it with someone, Totie might not get it for days."

So not only did I have to parade through the Riviera, I had to repeat the process at the International. At least there the staff saw the humor in the situation and smiled as we wended our way the length of the entire casino to the stage door. I felt safe enough leaving the chair with the stage manager, and my faith was justified when photographs were delivered about an hour later showing Totie Fields, who turned out to be a very short woman, perched regally on the chair, her feet dangling several inches above the floor.

Phyllis was delighted with her prank; Totie was thrilled with the chair; and I was relieved that the episode was finished.

Las Vegas turned out to be a lot of fun, as Karen had predicted. She and I settled into a pleasant routine of getting up about 10:00 A.M. and meeting for breakfast in the coffee shop. After breakfast we would check the mail, then go lie out by the pool until about 2:00 P.M., when I returned to my room to check in with Phyllis. If she wasn't in the mood to dictate or go through her mail, I spent the afternoon typing letters and making phone calls. At 7:30 P.M., Karen and I would meet Phyllis backstage, except on evenings when Warde wasn't around, in which case we'd go up to the suite and escort Phyllis through the kitchen to the dressing room. Warde particularly enjoyed Las Vegas when his friends visited. They would go out, sometimes not returning until just before show time when he had to make the announcement.

I loved John Davidson's act, and as soon as the orchestra began tuning up, I'd scamper downstairs to watch. Phyllis would have looked through the mail and as a rule she didn't need me to hang around. Helping her dress, doing her wig and getting her ready to go onstage was Karen's job.

John Davidson opened his act with "Joy to the World" (not the Christmas carol), and to this day every time I hear that song, I'm magically transported backstage to the Riviera Hotel in Las Vegas, smelling that wonderful smell of musty curtain and perspiration and perfume and marveling again at how the stage lights blind you to anything past the second row of the audience. If they didn't laugh or applaud, you wouldn't know there was anyone out there.

Between shows, Karen and I had dinner in the coffee shop while Phyllis and Warde ordered room service, either backstage or in their suite. At the end of the first week, Phyllis invited Karen and me to dinner with the two of them at a nearby Italian restaurant. I was ill at ease since we had an undefined relationship in social situations. I mean, were we still supposed to be working, or was this purely personal? Afterward we would be going back to work, so I didn't think we'd all be relaxed and happy.

However, it turned out to be quite pleasant. Several people stopped by to greet Phyllis, but for the most part she was left in peace. We had a delicious dinner, and I enjoyed the change from eating in the hotel. Warde didn't say much, and the atmosphere in the dressing room before the second show was almost convivial.

During the second week, I was lying by the pool when I heard someone mention "the earthquake in California this morning." As a native of the San Fernando Valley, I was used to quakes, which occurred from time to time, so I thought nothing of it until I passed the newsstand on the way to my room.

"Major California Quake!" a headline screamed, followed by "Freeway Collapses!" on the second line. *Newspapers always exaggerate.* I just smiled when I overheard a couple exclaiming over the paper. *Obviously not westerners.* After I showered and dressed, I switched on the television as I sorted through the afternoon mail. The on-screen images featured ambulances with screaming sirens. *Yeah, yeah, must be a slow news day.* It did not perturb me until the announcer said, "The phone company has asked that you not try to call your friends in the San Fernando Valley. The phone lines are down."

I stared at the screen for a moment as his words sank in, then lunged for the phone to call my parents. I dialed several times but only got a fast busy signal indicating trouble on the line. I tried to tell myself that the press was just playing it up as they always do.

Then the phone rang. My parents. They wanted to reassure me. The quake was nowhere near them, nothing was broken, no one was hurt. Of course, I'd known it all along, I told them, as I felt my breathing return to normal.

That weekend, Las Vegas got especially busy—a lot of people decided to put a few hundred miles between themselves and the San Andreas Fault.

15

We'd been back from Las Vegas only two days when I answered a call from Phyllis's agent. "Ask Phyllis if she'll fill in for Debbie Reynolds at the Desert Inn," he said without preamble. "Debbie's sick and needs a couple of nights off."

I was reluctant to buzz Phyllis. She might still be asleep. I did it anyway and she answered immediately.

"Mr. Moch wants to know if you'll go back to Vegas. He's on line two." In less than a minute, her voice came over the intercom.

"We're going to Vegas. Make reservations for the four of us."

It was the middle of the week, so there were plenty of open flights. Karen and I went home and packed, and agreed to meet at the airport at 3:30. Perry would drive Phyllis and Warde.

As I left the office, I picked up a handful of incoming mail, including pages of jokes that people had sent to Phyllis in hopes of selling them, and stuffed it all into my briefcase. Phyllis wrote about half of her material. The rest she bought from writers who sent in pages of one-liners. Phyllis read through them and circled any she wanted. She paid $5.00 a gag. Maria wrote the check and typed the gag on a 3x5 index card. Ingrid then filed it in Phyllis's huge card file. Comics are very possessive of their material. Once Phyllis bought a gag, she would be angry if she heard another comedian using it. That happened only a couple of times, and who knew whether it was an unscrupulous writer selling the same gag over again, or someone had simply appropriated her material for their own. Once she used a gag on television or it appeared in the newspaper, she took it out of her stage act.

"It's not fair to make people pay to hear jokes they already know," she said. She also tried to be very careful about which lines she used in interviews with writers who would quote her.

As we boarded the plane, I asked Phyllis, "What's wrong with Debbie, do you know?"

"Vegas Throat," she said.

It was the bane of singers in Las Vegas, caused by a combination of the arid climate, air conditioning, and smoke-filled showrooms. Put that together with two shows a night for two weeks with no nights off, and it was enough to push a singer who had been on the go for a long time right over the edge. The only cure was rest.

The limo from the Desert Inn met us at the airport for the brief drive to the hotel. Karen took the costumes and wig boxes directly to the dressing room while I checked us into our hotel rooms. Phyllis and Warde had already been escorted to their room by the hotel manager and, once again, my checking in was only a matter of form. I was pleased to find that Karen and I were in an entirely different wing from Phyllis and Warde.

I left our bags in our respective rooms and found my way backstage. Karen already had laid out Phyllis's make-up on one end of the dressing table and hung the costumes in the closet. Although we still had over an hour before the first show, we decided to wait for dinner until afterward. Between shows, Phyllis and Warde decided to have something in the dressing room, while Karen and I adjourned to the coffee shop. Service was slow, so by the time we were finished, we went straight backstage once again and got there just as the stage manager was calling "half hour."

We found Phyllis looking through the pages of submitted gags; she had circled several. She had also autographed cards that people sent and they were ready to be mailed. Phyllis was conscientious about that. Serious autograph collectors would send a pair of index cards and a self-addressed, stamped envelope. Some celebrities had their secretaries or someone else sign the cards, but Phyllis never did.

The dressing room felt claustrophobic with four people in it. I picked up the mail. "I'm going to drop these off," I told them as I left.

I dawdled through the beautiful casino, admiring the chandeliers and watching the elegant patrons playing at the gaming tables. When I returned, Phyllis had gone onstage, and Karen was absolutely livid, her face red and her voice shaking. She was one cool customer and I'd never seen her like this. Obviously something had gone very wrong.

"What's the matter?" I asked.

"You just won't believe it."

"What?"

"There was a call for Phyllis, and Warde actually put her on the line."

"And?"

"It was a threat."

"Oh, no." I felt sick. The call to the radio station in Pittsburgh leapt to mind.

"It was someone saying they've kidnapped Stephanie."
"Her daughter Stephanie?" I was horrified.
Karen nodded.
"What did they want? What did Phyllis say?"
"It was just before she went on. She almost fainted." Karen glanced at her watch for the tenth time. "C'mon, we need to be there when she comes off."
"Did you call the police?" I asked as we headed for the wings. Luckily the audience was laughing so much I could talk without being heard out front.
"Police?" Karen almost shouted at me. "No, I didn't call the police. I called Stephanie."
"And?"
"She was asleep."
"She's okay?"
"Of course she's okay. It was a hoax."
By that time Phyllis was saying "good night, I love you" to the laughing, shrieking audience as the orchestra struck up her jaunty play-off music. I couldn't hear what Karen said.
As soon as Phyllis got out of sight of the audience, she shouted over the noise of the orchestra. "Stephanie?"
"She's fine," Karen shouted back.
Even with her makeup on, I could see that the color had drained from Phyllis's face. "I want to talk to her," Phyllis said and began running toward the dressing room. In spite of the zany costume and red circus-pony feather sticking out of her hair, there was nothing comical about her at that moment.
I dialed the number while Karen undid Phyllis's costume. As soon as Stephanie answered, I handed the phone over.
"Stephy?" The relief in Phyllis's voice went right to my heart. "Honey, are you okay?"
I heard Warde outside and as the door opened, Karen

picked up her purse. "Let's get out of here," she growled as she brushed past me. I was right on her heels.

I couldn't believe someone would intentionally do something so horrible. I wondered if the person was sitting in the audience so he could watch Phyllis's reaction. I began to think being famous wasn't all that great.

The next afternoon, Karen and I went shopping at J. Magnin, the only department store on the Strip—conveniently located next door to the Desert Inn. I'd already discovered the monotony of being on the road, and it didn't often happen that there was anywhere to go outside the hotel. At the store I found a terrific white muslin caftan with black embroidery that I figured would be a perfect bathing suit cover-up. It was on sale at a bargain-basement price, and I snatched it up.

Once we'd combed the store from front to back and side to side, killing as much time as we could, we strolled back to the hotel to figure out what to do for the rest of the day. I'd already abandoned the idea of going out to the swimming pool; the temperature was only in the 60s. What a shame—I was eager to wear my new caftan. The show didn't start for another four hours, I didn't want to gamble, and there wasn't any work to be done, so when I heard myself paged, I cheered up.

"Madam wants to talk to you," Warde said after I answered the page. Somehow he always made it sound like a threat.

"Robin," Phyllis said after he handed her the phone, "Debbie says she's better and she's going to do her show tonight. I want you and Karen to get my things from the dressing room."

"Do I need to make plane reservations?" I asked.

"No, I think I'll stay over. She feels okay at the moment, but I'd hate to leave and then have her get sick again. They'd have to close the showroom."

It was only the second time I'd been in Las Vegas, but I already realized the importance of the shows. The showroom served as a conduit to draw people into the casino. Hotels didn't want their showroom dark for even one performance. Not only that, the shows were precisely timed so that when the show let out, the casino had its full complement of black-jack dealers and roulette and craps croupiers at the tables, ready for the crowd. A show that ran over by even a few minutes could lose the casino gambling revenue, so the entertainers were held to a strict schedule.

I found Karen at a slot machine and told her what Phyllis had said, so she cashed out her three dollars in winnings and we went backstage to pack up. By the time we got the bags to Karen's room, we had killed only an hour.

"What now?" I asked, but she didn't have any ideas, either. A boring afternoon and monotonous night loomed before us.

"Do you suppose I should make plane reservations in case she wants to leave after the second show?" I asked.

"Nah, we won't have any problem if she wants to leave tonight. There's never a problem getting *out* of Las Vegas on the weekend."

We sat in Karen's room with a pack of cards from American Airlines and played gin rummy. We always had a deck of cards with us. Karen liked to play and was a demon at cards. She beat me, as she always did. After we got tired of cards we decided to have dinner.

"We'd better check in with Phyllis one more time," Karen said.

I called Phyllis's room. Warde answered and told me that Debbie was still planning to do the show, but Phyllis had promised to stand by, just in case. I told him we'd be in the coffee shop. The restaurants were enticing, but too expensive for our $10 per diem.

As we sat down, I told Karen, "I don't care how much it costs, I'm going to have a steak." I glanced at the menu and ordered the New York strip with baked potato, veggies, and a side salad. The price was more than double the per diem, but it would be even more than that in the steak house, where the price covered the service, the atmosphere, and the ambiance. The food came from the same kitchen, and that was all I cared about.

Karen was not much of a meat eater and ordered fresh brook trout. I wondered where on Earth they got brook trout in the middle of the desert and very much doubted it was fresh.

"Fresh-frozen," the waitress confirmed.

Just as our food came I heard my name over the page.

"Don't answer," Karen advised.

"How can I not answer? They know I'm here."

"Pretend you didn't hear the page."

I knew that if I did that I wouldn't enjoy my meal. Reluctantly, I excused myself and went to the house phone. It was Warde, as I knew it would be.

"Are you eating yet?" he asked. I told him we had just been served. "Well, don't interrupt your dinner. We just wanted you to know that we're going to stay backstage for the show. When you're through eating you can come on back."

I didn't know if it was an invitation or a command. I told Karen, and we made dinner last as long as possible. I even ordered wine to go with my steak. I seldom drank, and never while working, but that wasn't exactly working.

By the time we got backstage, it was between shows and no one was around. We wandered back out to the casino, and I watched Karen feed a few dollars into a slot machine, but the machine didn't reciprocate and she walked away a little poorer. The second show would start at midnight and by 11:30 the joint was jumping. We decided it was time to go backstage.

The dressing rooms in Las Vegas were plush. They usually consisted of two rooms—a reception-type room with a bar and several chairs and couches, pictures on the walls, and a television. It almost looked like someone's living room. The actual dressing portion of the room was separate and fairly large, with a long, well-lighted dressing table and an entire wall of closets and shelves. An entertainer could have several people in her dressing room and still have her privacy by going into the inner room.

Phyllis and Warde were sitting in what I thought of as the living room portion of Debbie Reynolds' dressing room, talking quietly. Karen and I settled on the couch, waiting to find out what we should do. Debbie was in the inner room with her mother, brother, and daughter. Debbie's brother stepped into the living room, closing the door behind him. "Would you like to go out front and watch the show?" he asked.

Phyllis and Warde declined, and Karen wasn't interested, so I declined as well. I didn't want to sit out front by myself.

"Once the show starts," Phyllis told us, "you can watch from the wings if you like."

It wasn't long before the "five minute" call came over the speaker, followed by "two minutes to show time, ladies and gentlemen. Two minutes."

I'd never been really enamored with show business, but every time I heard that announcement, with the cacophony of the orchestra tuning up and the last check before the curtain went up, it made my heart beat a little faster. Somehow, it seemed magic.

We waited until Debbie went onstage, then Karen and I found a place where we could watch without being in the way. Debbie danced and sang, sashaying around the stage in a lovely, sparkly dress. After about a half hour she approached the audience.

"Do you mind if I sit down?" she asked as she sank gracefully to the floor and dangled her feet over the edge of the stage.

"Could I have a glass of water?" she called out toward the wings, and the stage manager came out with water and a towel.

"I'm exhausted," she confided to the audience. "I've been sick but thought I could make it through two shows. I hate to disappoint my audiences." Her smile beguiled and begged for indulgence.

About that time I became aware of a whispered argument going on behind me. I glanced around to see Debbie's mother and daughter, Carrie, who must have been about thirteen. The teenager seemed distressed.

"Please don't make me," she pleaded. "I don't want to do it."

"After all your mother has done for you!" the older lady remonstrated. "Here she is night after night knocking herself out. She's worked herself into a state of exhaustion, and she's doing it all for you. You have to help her."

"No, I don't want to."

I thought the girl was going to cry.

"You have to!" the grandmother said. "You have to help your mother."

I glanced at Karen. She'd heard the exchange, too.

Only a moment later, Debbie told the audience she would ask her daughter to come sing for them. The grandmother propelled Carrie, who looked frightened and clutched a guitar, into the spotlight. She sang a couple of songs, neither badly nor well, while her mother beamed from her perch at the edge of the stage.

I wondered what long-term effects, if any, the coercion and guilt would have on a child. I felt sorry for her and embarrassed that I'd overheard such a private conversation.

The show mercifully ended, and Karen and I went to find Phyllis and Warde. They were still in Debbie's dressing room, so we left them there and called it a night. We had reservations for a flight at noon the next day and nothing more needed to be done until morning.

As we checked out, the desk clerk scrutinized our bills before we signed them.

"No meals?" she asked.

"I beg your pardon?"

"You didn't eat while you were here? There aren't any meals charged."

"We paid cash."

"Oh," she said. "Didn't anyone tell you that your meals were comped? You didn't have to pay."

16

Phyllis had nothing on the schedule for the ensuing week, so when my friend Barbara invited me to come to San Francisco for a few days, I accepted. Barbara and I had been secretaries at the American Embassy in Pretoria and shared a flat for over two years. She'd quit the Foreign Service and moved to San Francisco a year before I left London. Barbara and I had a great time, going to the opera and visiting museums. I returned to Phyllis's a week later feeling totally refreshed.

The morning I got back, there was a flurry of activity, and I heard Val tell Maria, "They're going to come see her this afternoon."

"Who's coming to see her?" I asked Maria when we were upstairs in the office.

"Oh, it's some men who want to manage her."

"I thought Mr. B was her manager."

"He's her business manager," Maria said, "but these people want to manage her career."

"But she's got an agent. Why does she need a manager?"

"Well, the way I understand it," Maria began, "is that the agent works for the agency and they handle lots and lots of people."

The William Morris Agency was in fact the largest agency in the business at that time. Their office building teemed with agents and assistant agents and administrators and secretaries and all kinds of people bustling about, many wearing gold chains. I'd only been there once to pick up something for Phyllis, but I could readily believe that their main interest would be the agency rather than the client.

"The manager," Maria went on, "only has a few clients and he works for them. He goes out and gets bookings for them. The agent waits for the bookings to come to him, and then he finds the right client to fill the booking."

"Do they get 10 percent, too, or do they split it with the agent?"

"I'm not sure, but I think they get 10 percent, too."

It seemed to me that a lot of people were taking a percentage of Phyllis Diller—her agent, her attorney, and her publicist, and it looked as if there would be a manager, too. On top of that, she had to pay her staff and someone to handle her fan mail (the routine fan mail was answered by a professional who had stacks of pre-autographed pictures for that purpose) and her costume designer, Omar. What with all that and the expenses of keeping a house and family, I concluded show business wasn't quite as lucrative as I'd assumed.

Shortly after 3:00 P.M. I heard the doorbell ring, followed by a muted bustle and the buzz of the intercom.

"Mr. Gerber and Mr. Weiss are here to see Miss Diller," Val said. I found Phyllis in the Doris Day Room and told her the managers had arrived.

Phyllis came out and escorted them into the dining room, which was one of the few rooms in the mansion with doors that closed. The meeting went on for two hours. When they emerged, we nearly collided as I headed for the front door, on my way home. I gave them a quick look-over. They both impressed me, but why I couldn't really tell. The next morning, Phyllis called me to her room and said, "Roy Gerber and Norman Weiss are going to be my personal managers." She handed me two business cards and told me to add them to the Rolodex.

"I'm not sure I'm doing the right thing," she said, "but I'm going to give it a try. They say they can double my bookings."

That'll be fun, I thought. More places to see. I also figured that if they doubled her earnings, 10 percent of that would be very well spent.

Phyllis had scheduled a meeting with Roy Gerber, who worked in L.A. Mr. Weiss returned to his home in New York. When Roy came back to the house, Phyllis told me to sit in on the meeting. We met around the large table in the dining room.

"So, you play the piano?" Roy asked.

Well, you could hardly miss seeing the huge concert grand in the living room.

"Yes. Not as much as I'd like to," she said.

"Why not put that in the act?"

"I started my career by vamping around a piano. I used it as a prop and I don't need to anymore."

"But you sing."

"Yes."

"I've got an idea. How about ending your performance with a song?"

Phyllis squinted and looked off into the distance.

"You've already done Broadway," Roy said. "Why not use that song, the one about the parade?"

"*Before the Parade Passes By*," Phyllis said.

"Yeah, that one."

Because it had been barely a year since Phyllis had played the lead in *Hello, Dolly!*, she already knew the song and it was indeed a rousing number.

"It would be a terrific close to your show," he said.

Phyllis didn't answer right away. Finally, she shrugged. "Okay, let's try it."

Her lack of enthusiasm puzzled me, as if she didn't want to do any of it. I wondered if Mr. B had urged her to try something different.

She practiced the song and Roy had the music written out for the orchestra. As far as I was concerned it meant one more bag to count and a real rehearsal on every engagement, not only for the orchestra, but for the sound check and the lighting, too.

The first time Phyllis tried it, she was pleased with the audience's reaction. People actually stood and cheered as she reached the finale. Although her primary talent was certainly not singing, her enthusiasm and determination carried the day. *Parade* provided an exciting end to her performance. Somewhat grudgingly, I felt, Phyllis admitted that Roy had been right.

Once she felt comfortable with it in her show, Roy brought up the idea of the piano again. "How would you feel about performing with a symphony orchestra?"

"Concerts?" I asked Karen later. I couldn't imagine Phyllis Diller playing with a symphony. As it turned out, the idea wasn't as farfetched as it sounded. Celebrity appearances with an orchestra were becoming a fad. Danny Kaye was perhaps the most popular of these guest celebrities; he did talking numbers such as *Peter and the Wolf* or *Tubby the Tuba*.

Phyllis's first concert booking was with the Pittsburgh Symphony and its "pops" program. It turned out to be a happy mistake. They weren't aware that Phyllis actually played the piano, and Phyllis didn't realize they didn't know. She practiced two Bach études, then wrote a whimsical skit about a little old lady on a park bench to be done to her own composition, *The Diller Waltz*. She sent her program to the symphony manager, and apparently he thought her playing the piano was some kind of joke.

At the rehearsal, Phyllis sat down at the piano and began playing Bach. Few people knew she had once studied to be a classical pianist. Very quickly the noise in the auditorium abated as everyone, including the musicians in the orchestra, watched in astonishment as Phyllis Diller ripped through the Bach étude. When she finished, they rewarded her with enthusiastic applause. That was probably the most fun they'd had at a rehearsal in ages.

Meanwhile, I sat sewing together a "boa" out of moth-eaten fox pelts Phyllis had received from Goodwill, her pet charity.

When she had a break, I asked, "How do you want these foxes stitched?"

"I just want one long string of them so that it sort of drags on the floor."

"No, what I mean is, do you want them nose-to-tail or nose-to-nose?"

"Oh." She picked up a couple of pelts and tried them both ways. "What do you think?" she asked.

"Well, nose-to-nose is going to be a little awkward, but nose-to-tail is sort of obscene."

We both looked at the bedraggled pelts again.

"It'll look funny tail-to-tail and nose-to-nose, though," she mused. "No, I think nose-to-tail is how it's got to be." She held a pair of them up that way and broke into a huge laugh. "Maybe a little obscene," she said as she walked away.

So while she continued the rehearsal, I sat surrounded by a pathetic pile of pelts and stitched diligently. Ordinarily, it would be Karen's domain, but Karen had gone to a department store to buy a couple of yards of white material to add to the end of one of Phyllis's gloves so when the "little old lady" took off her glove it would seem to be miles long.

Phyllis had come up with all of this just before we left L.A. As show time approached, we worked frantically to pull it all together.

The audience that night had no idea what was going to happen. The first half of the concert was a regular symphony performance. After the intermission, the lights dimmed and the concert master walked onstage to applause. The orchestra conductor followed him to more applause. Then an announcer from backstage intoned, "Ladies and gentlemen, tonight we are honored to bring you the concert stylings of the legendary *Dame Illya Dillya!*"

Phyllis swept onstage wearing a stunning floor-length, blue-satin coat and a white fur stole around her neck. The audience applauded wildly. She then removed the stole and slowly took off her gloves. Finally, she unzipped the satin coat to reveal a magnificent white satin dress covered in beads and crystals. At this point the audience was in stitches and all she'd done so far was take off a few clothes. Then she sat down at the piano. No one expected funny-lady Phyllis Diller, with the houseful of unironed laundry and dumb kids, to actually sit down and play a concert grand.

As she herself admitted, her playing was not concert quality. She flubbed some notes, but that only made it funnier. When she hit an obviously wrong note, she laughed and the audience laughed with her. At first the conductor stopped and looked at her, but then he simply shrugged and the orchestra played on. The little old lady sketch did not go as well. There had been too little rehearsal, and Phyllis improvised as she went along. Cute at first, it soon started to drag and the audience grew restless. She later decided not to use it in her regular concert program, which I thought was a shame. It could have been a gem.

Phyllis practiced a lot more after that and her subsequent performances were better, but I never heard an error-free étude, and somehow I think everyone would have been disappointed with a perfect performance. When she made a mistake, she would turn to the audience with a "what did you expect?" kind of expression as if they were sharing an inside joke. Everyone had a good laugh.

Back in L.A., Phyllis's schedule started to fill up with conventions and state fairs as well as shows in Chicago, Indiana, Houston, and San Francisco. We went from an average of three weeks at home for every one on the road to just the opposite. I loved it. Traveling made me happy. At the end of April—had it really been four months since we were in London?—the schedule listed only one appearance between June 2 and July 12, a benefit in Los Angeles. A month later, Phyllis had seven new appearances between those dates: a week at The Music Circus in Sacramento, a celebrity game show in San Diego, a taping of *Love, American Style*, an appearance at Magic Mountain in California, hosting *The Tonight Show* in New York, and an entire week in London on the *Des O'Connor Show*.

Yes! And there was no debate about my going to London. I had proven that I could handle it. Besides, as Phyllis put it, I "spoke the language."

We went in early June, which was certainly preferable to December. Once again, I stayed at the Cumberland. Des O'Connor was an English comedian, but his show lacked the vitality of Tom Jones's show. Phyllis had two skits and we rehearsed them in the car on the hour-long ride to the studio. Once again, we passed the home for retired horses. It was so typically English that even Warde, on the days he went with us, got a huge kick out of it.

With only two skits and her monologue to tape, we had plenty of free time. Warde and Phyllis went out every night, and so did I. Once the limousine dropped me off at the hotel, I could do as I pleased. In June, it stayed light until long past dinnertime, and I loved strolling through Hyde Park in the extended summer twilight, savoring all the sights and sounds that were distinctly London.

The first night in town, I sauntered along Park Lane, enjoying the excitement of the great city. I promised myself that I would never have a plain old nine-to-five job again. Eventually, I reached the Dorchester Hotel, where I was meeting friends for dinner. I'd arrived early, so I went into the elegant lounge where Mary of Teck, wife of King George V, had taken afternoon tea from time to time. As I stirred my drink—not tea—a feeling of well-being washed over me, and I knew at that moment the snail was on the thorn, God was on His throne, and all was indeed right with the world.

It was just as well I couldn't see into the future, for it would surely have ruined a lovely evening.

The next day, the car arrived late; then I discovered I had forgotten my briefcase, so we had nothing to work on between takes. Des O'Connor made extensive changes to the skit with Phyllis, so the rehearsal dragged on. Warde paced the dressing room like a caged tiger because of the delays, which messed up their dinner plans, and when we did emerge from the studio, it was pouring rain.

When I finally got back to my hotel, I had a message from Tim, the friend I was supposed to have dinner with, saying he'd been called out of town. "Perhaps we could do it next time," the message read. Tim and I had been introduced by friends who thought we would make a great couple. We enjoyed many of the same things, and I loved his sense of humor, but the romantic spark was not there. I'd been looking forward to an evening of just kicking back with an old friend.

It was too late to call anyone else, and I didn't feel like leaving the hotel, especially now that the weather had turned cold as well as rainy. I hated eating out alone and room service was practically nonexistent, so I went down to the gift shop and bought a paperback novel for an outrageous price, got a candy bar for dinner, and returned to my room feeling miserable, hating every minute of being on the road and wishing I were back in California where it was sunny and I could at least pick up the phone and talk to someone.

The rain continued the rest of our stay. Of course, this should have been no surprise. In England it rained. In fact, when I'd lived there, I was always amused by visitors who remarked in the same sentence, "It's so beautiful and green, but it rains all the time." I always wanted to say, "Do you suppose that could be cause and effect?" So, yes, why should I be put out because of the rain? It wasn't logical, but I was.

On Friday, I checked out of the Cumberland and took a taxi to the Connaught. As I entered the suite, Phyllis was just hanging up the phone. "That was Colin. The airport is fogged in."

"What do you want to do, Ada?" Warde asked.

"We might as well head out there. Fog doesn't last forever." So we packed everything into the Rolls Royce and headed for Heathrow Airport, where I filled out the forms for customs and passport control. We sat in the VIP lounge for hours while the PSR issued occasional bulletins, telling us that nothing had changed—which we already knew by simply looking out the window. An impenetrable curtain of fog surrounded us.

Phyllis and Warde talked and drank copiously. I read and reread all the magazines and wished Karen were there.

As the afternoon dragged by, everyone in the lounge became short-tempered and edgy. At last, we heard the blessed sound of an airplane engine—someone was taking off. The fog had lifted! Or had it? The PSR announced that the fog had cleared just enough to get that one plane off the ground. It had been sitting on the runway for over three hours waiting for a break. I heard some talk in the lounge that we should be allowed to embark as well, but before it turned into a full-fledged mutiny, the PSR told us there would be no more flights that day. I got on the phone to Colin.

"I'll come right away," he said.

Next I called the hotels, dismayed to find they were both booked solid. The Connaught conceded that they might be able to find a room (not a suite, mind you) for Miss Diller, but that was the absolute most they could do.

"Couldn't you stay with friends?" Warde asked.

"I certainly could not!" I replied. The thought of calling someone on Friday night and announcing that I needed a place to stay was ludicrous. I had to bite my tongue to keep from saying something I would regret later. I wasn't there on vacation; I was working for Phyllis and it was up to her agent to find me a room.

By the time the Rolls arrived, all of us were tired and dispirited. Thank goodness for Colin's phlegmatic English temperament. Totally unruffled, he took charge of the situation. In the end, he'd managed to get me a room at the Connaught, although they still insisted they were booked solid.

We arrived at the hotel bedraggled and shopworn. Phyllis and Warde went directly to the dining room for dinner, but a concierge sent Warde to his room to get a tie—gentlemen wore ties in the dining room.

After I had seen to the luggage (Lord, it seemed that I was born counting bags!), I returned to my room and threw myself into the easy chair. The room was small but incredibly elegant compared to the modernized digs at the Cumberland.

I wouldn't mind eating my candy-bar dinner right here.

I checked the time. Still early, so I called Tim of the canceled dinner, even though I didn't hold out much hope for a spur-of-the-moment evening. Not only was he home, he was thrilled I was still in London.

"I'll pick you up in an hour," he said without even waiting to hear of the day's misadventure.

An hour later I'd showered and put on makeup and a nice dress, so I was ready when the desk called from downstairs. "A gentleman to see you," the operator told me.

I smiled as the elevator made its slow descent. Tim was indeed a gentleman, but I was quite certain that only "gentlemen" and "ladies" patronized the Connaught.

"Nice digs," he said as he held the car door for me.

"Believe me, this is not the norm!"

Tim took me to a delightful restaurant, one of many little places that he knew. I regaled him with stories of the week's work, and he told me he had never liked the *Des O'Connor Show* anyway. We had a simple dinner and a bottle of pinot noir. The perfect antidote to having spent the day in the airport lounge. As he talked, I looked at Tim wistfully. He reminded me of Paul McCartney, with his cute, cocky grin and his slightly untamed hair. *Why did we never become romantic?*

". . . she's a barrister's assistant."

"What? Who is? I'm sorry—I guess my mind was wandering."

"Jennifer. I was telling you. The girl I'm dating." His eyes crinkled and he grinned.

"Is this serious? Are you falling in love?"

"Not sure. I'll let you know." He poured the rest of the wine into our glasses. "You look like you're done in."

"It's been a long week."

Although the time was just past eleven, and I was indeed "done in," I was reluctant for the evening to end. I had a feeling that it was the end of an era. I was leaving London, perhaps for the last time.

"It's still foggy," I said as we stepped outside.

"Don't worry," Tim said. "It's never foggy two days in a row."

I knew he said that just to cheer me up. We arrived back at the Connaught and the doorman whipped open my door before Tim could get out of the car. Tim leaned across and gave me a hug. "It's been lovely," he said in that English accent I adored. It sounded "luv-lee."

I kissed him on the cheek. "Thank you."

We looked at each other for a moment, then he hugged me one more time. I slid out of the car and waved as he drove off in his little Morris Minor. In a matter of seconds, the fog had swallowed him up. I felt tears pricking behind my eyelids. *Good-bye, Tim. Have a nice life.*

I have no idea why I felt so melancholy that night. The horrendous day, the wine, the feeling that a chapter in my life had just come to an end, or maybe just exhaustion. I cried myself to sleep. The next morning dawned bright and sunny. My eyes were puffy, my hair was flat, and I really didn't give a damn. I just wanted to go home.

The Rolls picked us up on time, and Phyllis and Warde were subdued. We were all tired and ready for it to be over. At airport security, the guard started unpacking my purse. I had been shopping and seriously over-bought. Again. As a last resort, I'd crammed two bottles of my favorite English shampoo into my purse along with a couple of silk scarves from Liberty. Only with much adjusting and rearranging had I finally managed to zip it closed.

"Do you have to do that?" I whined as he extracted each item.

"Don't worry, young miss. I do this all day long." In no time he'd emptied my purse, then packed it all back so expertly that it zipped on the first try.

"Wow," I said. "I'm impressed."

He laughed. "When you do as many purses as I do in a day, you learn quickly."

Other than that, the trip back was long and boring. I tried to watch the movie, but it didn't interest me. Again I wished Karen were there so I'd have someone to talk to. It seemed to take forever to get to Los Angeles, then all at once we were there and it seemed as though we'd never been away. I couldn't believe it had ended so fast. Even on the drive home I dug out the schedule to see when our next trip would be.

17

After London, the highlight of the summer was Phyllis's two weeks at the Playboy Club-Hotel in Lake Geneva, Wisconsin. I'd never been to Wisconsin, but Karen raved about it.

"You're going to love it," she assured me. "It's just like Las Vegas, but green."

Unfortunately, Karen wasn't going. She had planned to visit her family in Hawaii long before this trip came up. Phyllis was reluctant to let her go, and Karen was particularly sorry to miss two weeks in Wisconsin. (When she first began talking about Lake Geneva, I had harbored a weak hope that she might, just possibly, be talking about Switzerland. I was glad that I had not said anything out loud when I found out it was Wisconsin.)

Karen had a compelling reason for sticking to her vacation plans. Her brother was getting married and she was in the wedding. She assured me I would have a good time, and I looked forward to it, although with some apprehension. The Playboy Club-Hotel conjured up images of scantily clad "bunnies" being chased around the pool by horny old codgers. When we arrived I saw children scampering about the lobby.

"We're a family hotel," the manager said as he showed us to our rooms.

The hotel sat in the midst of acres of landscaped grounds. My room, which was decorated in forest green and dark wood paneling, looked out on the golf course. The bathroom had lots of mirrors—maybe too many, I thought, as I struggled to zip up my slacks. The one drawback was that my room was right next to Phyllis's suite and our terraces abutted. No way would I be sitting outside enjoying the view with the possibility of one of them opening their sliding glass door and stepping out next to me.

As I hung up the last of my clothes, the phone rang.

"How do you like it?" asked Phyllis.

"Nice."

"Are you all unpacked?"

"Pretty much."

"Then let's go down to the Cabaret," the showroom where she'd be performing.

Finding the backstage entrance in any showroom is sometimes a puzzle. Often there is a discreet door opening right off the stage, sometimes the entrance is through the kitchen, and once in a while there's a separate entrance entirely. The Cabaret had an inconspicuous door right beside the stage. Phyllis had been there before, so she knew exactly where she was going.

When we'd first arrived, I'd told the bellman to take Phyllis's costume bags to the dressing room. There they all were, waiting to be unpacked. I unlocked them, Phyllis took out her wigs, and we both began hanging up the costumes and laying out the accessories. In no time at all we had everything ready.

"Almost as if Karen had done it," Phyllis remarked as she surveyed the neatly arranged rows of false eyelashes, the large pocket watch, the lipsticks, cigarette holders, and dog collars. We'd arrange the gloves by pairs in the drawers and the boots underneath the correct costumes, with the headdresses on the shelf above.

"Yeah, almost."

"Don't worry, you'll soon make friends here," Phyllis said. It was as though she had read my mind. She looked at the schedule and added, "Two shows a night, but you'll have your days free. Maybe you can learn to play golf. Or tennis."

Not a bad idea.

We had only a short time before the first show, so I went back to my room and set up the "office" on top of the dresser—my typewriter, a stack of typing paper, and a package of Phyllis's current favorite stationery, along with paper clips, scratch pads, Scotch tape, and stapler. From my briefcase I took my shorthand notebook and a couple of pens. I also had scratch pads and pens in different colors for the dressing room, the way Phyllis liked it.

Karen wasn't there, so I helped Phyllis with her costume. As we worked, I enjoyed listening to the singer—a young woman from Chicago. She had a good voice and a great figure, and fit much more into the style of what I thought a Playboy Club should have as entertainment. Phyllis Diller just didn't fit the Playboy vision, as far as I could see.

Between shows that first night, Phyllis and Warde would have dinner in their room. As the first show wound up, Warde said, "You should try one of the gourmet rooms. The food is fantastic."

"I hate to eat by myself."

He glanced at me with his lopsided grin, which looked very close to a leer. "I'm sure you could meet some nice gentleman who would be delighted to buy you dinner."

Warde was attempting to be nice, so I just smiled and shrugged. I wandered around, looking at the shops. There were some nice places to spend money, no doubt about that. There were also several places to eat. But in the end, I bought some crackers and cheese at the little "country store" and wished there were someplace to get fresh fruit. Phyllis's suite had a fruit basket, but nothing in the dressing room where I could get to it.

By the end of the second show, I practically fell asleep on my feet. Traveling without Karen made it harder—I was responsible for everything. We'd had a three-and-a-half-hour flight, a worse-than-usual time at the airport corralling all the bags, then the hour's drive to Lake Geneva. After Phyllis and I got the dressing room set up, I was ready for a break, but by then we were getting ready for the first show.

Besides that, the first night was always tense, when anything that could go wrong would go wrong, but thank heaven, it hadn't that night. When I got back to my room, I threw my clothes over the chair, told the hotel operator not to ring my room under any circumstance, and dropped into bed.

I slept until noon. It must have been the fresh air—people from L.A. weren't used to breathing fresh air. When I woke, I noted that the message light on my phone wasn't blinking. *Thank heaven.* I showered and dressed as quickly as possible and headed for the coffee shop. I wanted to get out of there before I got a call from next door. Oh, my gosh, did that breakfast taste good. I hadn't even eaten lunch the day before, and those cheese and crackers had been a sparse dinner. I felt life seeping back into my veins, via my stomach.

I went outside to explore. I strolled around the golf course until some angry golfer, who had been yelling "fore" for about thirty seconds, finally started speaking English and yelled, "Get outta the way!" I realized I was standing right in the middle of the fairway. Burning with humiliation, I retreated to the path.

I put as much distance between myself and the golf course as possible and ended up at the tennis courts on the other side of the hotel. Beyond that I saw an airstrip. Some people rode by on horses and it looked like they were having a good time. For just an instant I regretted that horses and I shared a mutual antipathy.

When I was a Girl Scout, our entire troop aimed for the "horsemanship" badge. We learned to ride—or at least the rest of them learned—at Verdugo Stables near my house in North Hollywood. I remembered being pointed toward a large, brown animal that towered over me. It looked at me with total disdain, and there was no doubt it was thinking, "This little pip-squeak thinks she can tell me what to do?" I mounted the horse as instructed and held the reins the way the riding master demonstrated.

"The first thing you want to do," he told us, "is let the horse know who's the boss." I swear that horse snickered. He turned his head toward me and we locked eyes. No contest. After a few turns around the paddock, we headed out onto the bridle trail. It took all of three minutes for that horse to dump me and trot right back to the stable. The riding master scowled at me; nor were my parents pleased when they had to take me to the emergency room to treat a badly sprained ankle. I concluded that horses are much better in concept than horses in reality.

The tennis looked interesting, though. *Lessons might be in order.* Karen and I had taken our racquets to Las Vegas, although neither of us played well, and she'd urged me to pack mine for this trip. "You're going to have a lot of time there. Maybe you'll find someone to play tennis with," she said.

As I returned to my room thinking of tennis, the first thing I saw was the blinking message light. *Drat.*

For a moment I thought about ignoring it but figured I might as well find out what Phyllis wanted. She wanted to work. *Double drat.*

Reluctantly, I went next door with my shorthand notebook. We spent the rest of the afternoon answering mail, with Phyllis dictating replies—some serious, some humorous—to both business and personal mail. I knew what I'd be doing the following morning—typing letters. Once we finished, it was time to dress and get down to the Cabaret.

Between shows that night the stage manager poked his head into the dressing room. "I just wanted to let you know what a pleasure it is to have you here, Miss Diller."

Phyllis, like everyone else, is not unappreciative of compliments. We had nearly half an hour before the next show started, so she invited him in.

"You and your secretary are such ladies," he continued, "and so professional. It's really a pleasure working with people like you."

We all chatted for a few minutes, then he looked at his watch. "Gotta call fifteen minutes," he said as he got up. The door closed behind him.

"Well," Phyllis remarked, "he certainly does like you."

"He does?"

"I don't think it's me he's interested in."

I hadn't paid particular attention to him, but, yeah, he was a rather nice-looking man about my age.

"Maybe he'll ask you to dinner," Phyllis suggested. She was by nature a matchmaker and always pleased when she thought I had a little romance going.

As it turned out, the entire stage crew and hotel staff were friendly. They were all as shy of me as I had been of them. They thought that because I worked for a celebrity and traveled a lot I would be stuck-up. The stage manager, Harvey, was attentive whenever we were backstage, but he never made a move to ask me out. Of course, the fact that we both worked nights sort of put the kibosh on that. When Phyllis was onstage, I hung out with him and learned that he'd lived in Wisconsin all his life, divorced with two kids who lived with his ex. Nothing serious, just a nice guy who liked to chat. Everyone at the Playboy Club-Hotel seemed really nice. The resort sure wasn't what I'd expected.

Despite its name, the only bunnies in the Playboy Club-Hotel were in the Cabaret or the bars; the place was not the showcase for scantily clad women I'd anticipated. We were out in the country, and there were no interviews or appearances other than her twice-nightly show, so Phyllis chose to spend part of every afternoon working with me, a goal she always strived for but seldom achieved—until then. I'd scheduled tennis lessons for the first time in my life. I knew I would enjoy learning to play. However, I spent a good part of every day either with Phyllis or back in my room typing correspondence. By the end of the week I'd hardly had a chance to get outdoors at all. I canceled the tennis lessons.

Some vacation. Wait till I get hold of Karen!

On Mondays, the Cabaret was dark, and Phyllis was booked for an appearance on the *Irv Kupcinet Radio Show* in Chicago. We took a small plane that used the airstrip behind the tennis courts. The woods came very close to the airstrip on one side; the other side was bordered by a cow pasture.

"What do you do if the cows wander onto the strip when you're trying to land?" Phyllis asked the pilot as we took off.

"I buzz the field, try to scare them off. Or else I hope someone will see I'm trying to land and come shoo them away."

"I suppose at night you could put flashlights in their mouths and line them all up alongside if you wanted to come in after dark," she suggested.

This struck the pilot as wonderfully funny, and he laughed so hard I was afraid the plane would crash. "Tell you what," he said when he'd caught his breath, "on the way back I'll fly you over the nudist camp."

"There's a nudist camp out here?" Warde had suddenly come alive.

"Sure is. Only thirty miles or so from the hotel. Way out in the woods."

True to his word, the pilot took a slight detour on the return flight and we made a low pass over a compound that he assured us was full of nude people. From our height it was impossible to tell if the few people lying around the pool were nude or not, but we all pressed our noses to the windows as he made another pass.

We got back at dusk, and Phyllis and Warde went immediately to their suite to change for dinner. One of the Playboy bigwigs had invited them to dine with him in the gourmet room.

When I got to my room, I had a message to call Diane, one of the front-desk clerks.

"Oh, good," she said when I identified myself. "I was hoping you'd get back soon. We're all going into town for dinner. Meet us in the lobby at seven. Mr. Hefner's buying."

Oh my gosh. Dinner! In a restaurant! With people!

I was in the lobby by seven. Earlier, actually. I didn't want to take a chance. I was so excited to be getting out. *This is pathetic,* I told myself.

Eight of us gathered, including Diane and two others from the front-desk staff. I didn't know the other four, all men. Diane introduced us, but I was still hazy. They worked somewhere around the hotel, but I really didn't care. I just knew I was going out to dinner.

"What about Harvey?" I asked.

"He never comes in on Monday. It's his night off," Diane said.

Didn't matter. I'd have had a terrific evening if I'd been with Dracula and the Abominable Snowman.

We went to an old ranch-style place that specialized in steaks. I didn't expect that Hugh Hefner would be there in person (and certainly would have been startled if he had!), but Diane's assurance that he was buying encouraged me to jump in with several of the others who ordered the biggest steak on the menu. When it came I caught my breath. The thing covered the entire plate—the potato and veggies were served on the side.

"You'll never be able to eat it all," one of the girls said. The really embarrassing thing was that I knew I could. The talk turned inevitably to my job.

"What's it like working for Phyllis Diller?" somebody asked.

This was something everyone wanted to know.

"She's great," I told them. "And I really like the traveling."

"I've never been further than Chicago," one of the girls said. "Have you ever been to a foreign country?"

"I've been to London with Phyllis twice."

She looked at me with such yearning that I didn't have the heart to tell her I'd lived there and in South Africa.

"Someday I'm going to London," she said.

I thought she sounded rather wistful. "What's it like working at the Playboy Club-Hotel?" I asked. "I gotta tell you, it's not at all what I figured."

One of the guys had just finished putting away most of that huge steak. "Yeah, it's not what most people think," he said.

"It really is a family destination," someone else said.

"So, what other celebrities have you had?" I asked.

"Oh, gosh, lots. George Gobel, Diahann Carroll, Dyan Cannon, Cyd Charisse. Just lots and lots."

"Those were the nice ones," another added, "but not

everyone's as nice as that. Some of them are really arrogant and just downright nasty. But you guys are the best."

I was happy to hear that and knew Phyllis would be, too.

When I returned to my room, I thought about some of the things they'd said. Phyllis was demanding and not always in a good mood, but she had plenty of good qualities. She didn't use foul language, she didn't throw temper tantrums, she could be generous when it suited her, and mostly gave credit where it was due. She was invariably pleasant to the people we worked with, and she tried to remember to give Karen and me free time when we were on the road. I had it pretty good.

As if to validate my kind thoughts, Phyllis suddenly lost her desire to work, so my remaining days were marvelously free. I put them to good use on the tennis court, taking lessons for the rest of the week. I was just starting to get the hang of it when it was time to pack up and head for home.

The last night the stage manager gave me a present—a cut-crystal egg with the Playboy bunny etched into it. "This is from all of us," Harvey said. "You've been so much fun. We just wish everyone were as nice as you and Miss Diller."

I keep it as a reminder of all the friends I made across the country, most of whom I will never see again.

18

Monday morning we packed up and left the Playboy Club-Hotel in Lake Geneva. I felt sort of sad. It had turned out to be a good time, as Karen predicted.

I'm gonna put those tennis lessons to good use, I told myself as I settled into my seat on the airplane. It was fun, and a tennis racquet was a lot more portable than a set of golf clubs.

I actually slept on the plane, which was good, because with the two-hour time change I still had an afternoon's work ahead of me. Maria was happy to have me back and eager for all the news. Like Phyllis, she always hoped that I would "meet someone nice." I don't know what good that would've done. In all likelihood I'd never see him again.

"You have to get ready for Las Vegas," she told me as she opened the office bags. Maria was very proprietary about the office bags. "You leave day after tomorrow."

She immediately began replenishing supplies, mostly the photos and books Phyllis used as thank-you gifts.

Maria kept talking to me—or perhaps herself—as she checked both staplers. "I must fill those up," she said, setting them aside. She carefully wrapped a rubber band around a box of paper clips. "You have to be careful about the paper clips. If the rubber band comes loose, they get all over the suitcase."

"Okay. I'll be more careful."

"How do you go through so many scratch pads?" she asked.

"No idea."

"I'll have to order more. Did you like the Playboy Club-Hotel?"

I filled her in on the overall picture.

"I'm glad you had such a good time. It's good that you enjoy the travel." Maria apparently had no desire to go anywhere but between her apartment and Phyllis's house.

That evening at home I emptied my suitcase and stuffed two weeks' worth of dirty clothes into the washer. The next day, Phyllis taped a *Sonny and Cher Show* in L.A. Thankfully, Karen had returned from Hawaii and went with her, so I was able to spend the day organizing the correspondence that had come in while we were gone.

Las Vegas would not be hectic, and I had begun to really enjoy the travel-with-no-work gigs. *If we could just spend all our time in Las Vegas, I'd be a very happy secretary!*

I verified the plane and limo reservations and made sure I had the contract in my briefcase. A quick glance at the contract told me the Riviera was paying Phyllis $50,000 a week. *A week!* That was more money than I would earn in many years. She told me not to discuss it with anyone, which made me think that she was being paid more than other entertainers—something, perhaps, the hotel wouldn't want known in that very competitive business.

My suitcase held all my summer clothes and a couple of bathing suits. August isn't the choice time to be in Las Vegas unless you want to spend all your time by the pool or gambling, both of which are best done in moderation. Phyllis and Warde stayed in the house she owned. It was nothing like the mansion in L.A., just an ordinary three-bedroom home on a nondescript street in an unassuming neighborhood.

Phyllis decided that Karen should stay at the house with them, which Karen hated. I hated that, too. It meant that unless she took a taxi and came to spend the day at the hotel, she was stuck in the house, and I was kicking around by myself.

One day Phyllis told Karen she could have the car for the day. Karen called me at the hotel.

"I'll pick you up in twenty minutes."

I waited in the air-conditioned vestibule and dashed outside as I saw the car pull up.

"Where to?" Karen asked.

"What about going out to Lake Mead?" I suggested.

We had only a hazy idea of how to get there. We found a street called Lake Mead Boulevard and foolishly assumed we would end up at Lake Mead. After three hours of driving through the desert, we gave up and headed back to the Riviera, thoroughly frustrated and unhappy. We never got even a glimpse of the lake.

Although the temperature was always well over 100 degrees, I spent part of each afternoon by the pool. Boy, did I get a great tan! When I got back to L.A. and my mother saw me, she gasped and suggested I stay out of the sun for the rest of the year. Looking at the photos later, I could see why she reacted as she did—I looked like a whole different person.

John Davidson again opened for Phyllis. I stood in the wings nearly every night to watch his show. Sometimes he stopped by Phyllis's dressing room afterward, but he never stayed long. Occasionally I saw him out by the pool with his wife and son. I concluded that, like me, he was a "day" person who got trapped in the wrong time slot.

After returning from Las Vegas, we left almost immediately for Missouri, where Phyllis played a fair in Sedalia. John Davidson was entertaining there, too, and just seeing the familiar faces of his band and his manager made it special. In Las Vegas, we'd been nodding acquaintances, but out in this "foreign place," his roadies and I became best friends. Between shows we ate hot dogs and cotton candy and wandered around the fair, looking at the prize livestock and playing the midway games. Whenever one of them won a prize—a stuffed animal or big beach ball—they'd turn around and give it to some kid who was passing by. Really, what would any of us do with a suitcase full of stuffed animals?

By the time we got back to L.A., I was exhausted. We had been traveling almost continuously since early June, when we'd gone to England. There'd been only one two-week break, and there was another full schedule ahead of us. For someone who liked to travel, I had a hard time coming to grips with the knot in the pit of my stomach as I glanced at all the new dates.

In September we had a ten-day tour of U.S. Air Force bases in Texas, with only one day off and sometimes two shows a night at different locations. Two days after that, Phyllis appeared at the Circle Star Theatre in San Carlos, California, for a week. Then a week in Chicago, and in the middle of that she had an afternoon appearance in Milwaukee for the American Horticultural Society. (We took a private plane that got us in and out for the hour-long performance and back just in time for Phyllis to go onstage in Chicago.)

At least we had a couple of weeks off in October before she went back to the Holiday House in Pittsburgh. At that point I would have been with Phyllis for an entire year. It was time to take a vacation, but the last thing I wanted was to get on a plane and go somewhere. Just hanging out at home sounded wonderful. I'd sleep late, go shopping, maybe take in an opera at the L.A. Music Center, and visit a couple of friends I hadn't seen in a while. Oh, yeah, that was exactly what I needed, and that's exactly what I did for an entire week.

19

During the time I worked for her, Phyllis made two television commercials—one for the Milk Board and one for Lipton Cup-A-Soup. The milk commercial was filmed at her home, one of a series featuring celebrities drinking a glass of milk and assuring viewers that "You never outgrow your need for milk." The strange thing was that they taped the commercial just before Phyllis had her famous face-lift, but she looked so good that people assumed the commercial had been made afterward. Which all went to prove a point: a good makeup artist can work miracles.

Phyllis had found an absolute wizard and insisted that whenever she appeared on television he did her makeup. I would have been more astonished at the transformation were it not for the fact that when I lived in London I had gone to Guerlain for a facial and had my makeup professionally done by a French lady who transformed me into the most beautiful thing I had ever seen in a mirror. The astonishing part was that when she finished, I didn't look made up at all. So when Phyllis's artist finished with her and the milk commercial aired, it did not surprise me to hear people comment how well Phyllis looked after her face-lift. They didn't know the commercial had been taped two weeks before.

When Phyllis decided to have a face-lift, her publicist, Frank, almost had apoplexy.

"You'll ruin your image!" he protested.

"Frank, I'm tired of having bags under my eyes. Pretty soon they'll be so big that the airline will charge me for extra luggage!"

While Phyllis laughed uproariously, Frank sputtered ineffectually. "You're not supposed to be pretty!"

"Nonsense!" she said. "People see what they want to see. When I tell them I'm ugly and flat-chested, they believe me."

"Well, maybe they won't realize there's a difference."

"Oh, no, Frank. I'm going to publicize it. I want you to put out a press release."

"What?" I judged that Frank was very near to having a stroke. "Phyllis, you can't do that," he said. "You're crazy. People don't talk about having face-lifts. It's like . . . it's as bad as . . ." He stumbled around searching for an analogy.

"Well, I'm going to be the first."

". . . as having a sex change!" Frank finished, adamant although not exactly triumphant.

"Frank, think of the publicity."

"I *am* thinking of the publicity."

"The first celebrity to admit to having a face-lift. Not only admit," Phyllis exulted, "but to publicize it! People have been doing it for years and I'm going to be the one to bring it out of the closet!"

"It'll be a disaster."

The argument raged back and forth, but it was a foregone conclusion that Phyllis would get her way. Frank just had to get used to the idea.

It took a while.

But as usual, Phyllis was right. The publicity did a great deal more good than harm, and I think the face-lift did as much for her morale as it did for her looks. It also became a wonderful topic of conversation on talk shows and for magazine articles. She even used it in her stage act.

20

Lipton Cup-A-Soup was then a brand-new product. Two thirty-second spots were to be taped the same day. I don't know what I expected, but I certainly didn't anticipate it being an all-day affair. I mean, it's only for thirty seconds, right?

When we arrived at the studio—a nondescript building in Hollywood—I was surprised to see it full of people. Not only were there the crews for the camera, lights, and sound, there was the grip, the prop man, and the script girl, as well as the director. Add to that, two account executives from the advertising agency for Lipton, a couple of people from the soup company, and of course Phyllis's agent from the William Morris Agency. Roy Gerber, her manager, came by for a few minutes, too. When Phyllis, Warde, Karen, and I arrived, the little studio almost certainly exceeded occupancy limit. I hoped the fire marshal wouldn't decide to drop in.

The set was a breakfast bar at which Phyllis would sit and extol the virtues of Cup-A-Soup in front of a flat that looked like the interior of a kitchen. Behind the cameras were a couple of rows of chairs where the entourage could sit and watch.

I accompanied Phyllis and Karen to the tiny dressing room but quickly realized I would be underfoot there, so I went back to the studio. Karen came out with an armload of Phyllis's costumes and stood in front of the breakfast bar. She held up one costume after another for the director to choose.

"Too glittery," he said, and condemned another with "bad color." On it went until a costume had been chosen. Phyllis, meanwhile, was being made up for the camera and Warde talked to her agent. Finally, Phyllis came out and the cameraman got his turn. "I'm getting too much glare off that dog collar," he shouted to someone—I had no idea who. The script girl produced a can of spray something-or-other that cut the glare.

"Smells awful," Phyllis said as Karen hooked the still shiny but not so sparkly piece of costume jewelry back in place.

Satisfied at last, the cameraman and the director began the walk-through. "Okay, quiet everybody," the director called.

"Quiet, everyone," his assistant echoed.

"Quiet on the set!" the script girl hollered.

I thought it would have gotten quiet a lot sooner if everyone hadn't been yelling for quiet.

The script called for Phyllis to pick up the box of soup from the kitchen counter, walk to the breakfast bar, enumerate the virtues of the soup that "cooks up in a cup instantly!" while the scene cut to a close-up of hot water being poured into a cup. Phyllis did not do the actual pouring—that had been taped earlier. By a professional water-pourer, I imagined. Phyllis would then pick up the mug of steaming soup and pronounce it "Delicious!" The cup would not have hot soup in it—just a small chunk of dry ice in the bottom of the cup to give the steaming effect.

As soon as the walk-through started, I began to appreciate the intricacies of taping a commercial.

"I'm getting too much swish from the dress," the sound man called. The beads on the dress clashed as she walked. Onstage that little bit of noise would not be noticeable, but in the recording studio the sensitive microphone picked up every slight sound. The director went into a huddle with Phyllis and Karen. They settled on the dress that the director had originally rejected as the wrong color. Instead of beads it had fringe.

Phyllis changed costumes and the rehearsal continued. As she reached the breakfast bar, she was to perch on one of the bar stools. However, no matter how she tried, the business of hoisting herself onto the stool looked clumsy.

"Why don't you just stand there?" the director suggested. That had to be cleared with the ad execs who had written the commercial and the Lipton people, who never spoke another word the entire day. They agreed, the bar stools were removed, and the rehearsal continued.

"I'm getting too much glare from the box of soup," the cameraman called as Phyllis held up the box.

"Try tipping it down just a little," the director said. Phyllis tipped it down a little and the results were satisfactory, but each time they did a "take" after that, the cameraman had to keep saying "more down," or "more up" to get the exact angle.

Phyllis's line, "The soup that cooks up in a cup instantly," took a lot of work. It's difficult to say quickly and distinctly. I had already learned from Phyllis that anything to be taped called for immaculate diction. Ordinary speech over the airwaves sounds mushy. Every letter has to be precisely spoken and *p*'s are especially difficult. Then, to say it with a perky smile and convey the idea that one has just discovered something as amazing as the Hope Diamond isn't easy—especially after the tenth time.

They tried it several different ways—first, with a little pause before the word "instantly," then with more emphasis on the word "soup," then switching the emphasis to the word "cup," and on and on. It seemed that they had just begun when the script girl announced the lunch break. At that point the entire group adjourned to a restaurant across the street, where reservations had been made. I was beginning to be concerned about the wisdom of breaking for a long lunch when the first of the two commercials hadn't even been taped. I needn't have worried, however. Everyone came back from lunch refreshed and the atmosphere in the studio, which had started to get a bit tense, was a lot more relaxed.

The commercials were finished on time.

"That went smoothly," I heard the grip tell one of the cameramen as everyone packed up. I hated to think what a difficult commercial would be like if those two thirty-second spots took an entire day's shooting.

When we reached the Rolls, Phyllis and Warde slid into the back seat while Karen stowed the suitcases in the trunk and I fished for the keys. Karen and I both hated driving the Rolls. Karen didn't like to drive at all, and I wore glasses to drive but hadn't carried them with me since I only used them in my car and that's where I kept them. Usually Warde drove, but that night he didn't want to. Karen and I held a brief conference across the trunk of the car and Karen lost. Triumphantly, I tossed her the car keys and climbed into the passenger seat. As she got behind the wheel, she stuck her tongue out at me.

It had been a long day, but things had gone well and everyone seemed satisfied. However, the spots would not be shown on the West Coast. I hoped to catch it on TV when we traveled to another city. I never did see it.

21

Next stop, Philadelphia. I'd never been there and looked forward to seeing the sights even though I knew we probably wouldn't have much free time. Phyllis had a one-day appearance in New York first, then a free day in between before she opened in the City of Brotherly Love. She used that time to visit her daughter Sally, who had mental problems and had been institutionalized for most of her adult life. A few people knew about this, but we were instructed to answer any inquiries about her with "Sally is in school in the East." Many years passed before Phyllis acknowledged Sally's problem publicly. When I worked for her, it was a secret.

After the New York visit, Phyllis, Warde, and Karen drove to Philadelphia in a rental car. I flew directly from L.A. and met them there.

It was the first time since I started working for Phyllis that I'd traveled without her and felt positively exhilarated at being on my own. The morning of the trip I got up and went straight to the airport without having to fret about meeting them, or having to prod Warde into being on time. There would be no passenger service representative to contact and none of the usual hassle of preboarding. I didn't have to worry about riding herd on a score of suitcases or filling out "tip slips," which Phyllis kept for tax purposes. I could just check in like any other passenger. I felt like a kid on holiday.

I arrived in Philadelphia in the early evening and took a taxi straight to the hotel. I had expected them to be there, but they weren't. *This is good. It will give me time to get settled before they show up.* I registered the three of them and, as usual, got an extra key to each room.

It was snowing in Philadelphia, and anyone who has been raised in Southern California will understand how exciting that was to me. I sat in my room with the lights off and watched the large flakes drift down. As the hours went by, however, I began to get apprehensive. The plan had been for them to get there about the same time I did. The next day Phyllis had two radio interviews and a rehearsal before the opening performance. It would be hectic at best, and if they didn't arrive soon, I knew Phyllis would be tired and grouchy in the morning.

I finally heard a commotion in the hall close to 9:00 P.M. Sure enough, the bellman was wheeling a large cart piled high with bags. I spotted two fur-draped people and Karen following them. (Phyllis had given Warde a full-length black mink coat. She said it was just like the one Elizabeth Taylor had given Richard Burton, and if Richard Burton could wear a mink coat, so could Warde. I must admit that he carried it off well.)

I ignored Phyllis and Warde, who were clearly in a bad mood, and fell in step beside Karen, who had already yanked her single bag off the top of the cart and was heading for her room just past mine.

"Why are you so late?" I asked as we stepped into her room.

"Oh, you know Warde," she replied, her voice heavy with sarcasm.

"I thought you'd be here hours ago."

"We got lost."

"How could you get lost between New York and Philadelphia? Isn't there a turnpike all the way?"

"He took a wrong turn."

By then Karen had slung her suitcase onto the bed and was studying the room-service menu.

"Have you had dinner?" she asked.

"No, I was waiting for you."

"Room service is probably going to take an hour." She tossed the menu aside. "I wonder if the dining room is still open." She called the hotel operator, who told her the dining room was closed but that she could order from room service.

We agreed to order something that they could fix in a hurry and settled on sandwiches and milk. A far cry from the nice dinner I'd been looking forward to after my two airline meals.

"So, how could you get lost?" I asked when Karen returned to her unpacking.

"After Warde took the wrong turn, he wouldn't pull off for directions. Phyllis kept telling him he was going the wrong way, and all he said was 'But, Ada, we're making such good time.' "

"That's an old joke, Karen."

"It's no joke!" she said with such vehemence that I immediately shut up.

I sat in silence and watched her arrange everything in her meticulous way and wished the food would get there. When it came, the sandwiches were neatly cut into fours, like a club sandwich, and arranged around a pile of potato chips accompanied by olives and pickles. It took us all of four minutes to devour everything.

"What time do we have to leave here tomorrow?" Karen asked as she stacked the empty plates on the tray.

"The first interview is at noon. We should leave here at eleven thirty." I'd asked at the desk when I checked in for directions to the radio station and the approximate driving time. "I'll call you when I get up."

"Don't make it early." Karen was more than just tired. Things had obviously not gone well the past couple of days. She and Warde got on each other's nerves, and it was always worse when they were together for any amount of time, especially in close quarters. Driving from New York to Philadelphia in the snow and the dark and getting lost had probably been the *coup de grâce*.

I realized I hadn't checked with Phyllis to give her our morning departure time.

"Do you suppose they'll still be up?" I asked Karen.

"Probably. They haven't had dinner, either."

I rang their room and Phyllis answered. "Just wanted to let you know we have to leave here at eleven-thirty tomorrow for the twelve o'clock interview."

"Call me at ten-thirty," she instructed.

I hung up and said to Karen, "We're set."

"Call me for breakfast," she said, handing me the tray of empty dishes to set outside in the hall.

Before I went to bed, I called the hotel operator to leave a wake-up call, then set my alarm. I never entirely trusted either one of them, especially because everyone else relied on me to wake them up. I made a few notes on the pad beside my phone:

1. Call radio station to confirm interview and travel time.
2. Call second radio station to confirm 3:00 P.M. interview.
3. Call club to confirm rehearsal time.
4. Call Phyllis at 10:30.

The next day was as hectic as I had anticipated. With two interviews and a rehearsal, then the show, we were all totally drained. Fortunately, Phyllis had only one show opening night. We were back at the hotel by midnight. With no interview scheduled for the next day, things looked like they were going to smooth out.

On the way back to the hotel, Phyllis mentioned that she and Warde had friends coming up on Saturday, so Karen and I could take the day off and have the car. I turned to Karen, grinning and silently clapping my hands. *Just what I'd been hoping for!* I wanted to visit Independence Hall and the Betsy Ross House and some of the other historic sights.

The next two days went well. Phyllis and Warde kept to themselves, so Karen and I saw them only when it was time to leave for the theater. On Saturday, Phyllis had several little errands for Karen to run before we took off with the car. It was after lunch before we finally got away from the hotel. We had to be back by 5:00 so it didn't make for a very long day off. Nevertheless, we did see Independence Hall and the Betsy Ross House, so I was content. I knew that if I had an ordinary job, I would have never even gotten to Philadelphia.

We left on Monday, and the trip home was uneventful but seemed unusually long. We got back to Phyllis's at six o'clock, and I was surprised to see the staff still there until I remembered it was only three o'clock California time.

I took the office bags upstairs and set them in the corner to unpack in the morning.

"How did it go?" Maria asked.

Briefly, I told her about the theater, Warde getting lost on the way from New York, and our truncated day off. "I saw Betsy Ross's house, though," I told Maria. Her blank stare reminded me that she was from Mexico. Maria then clucked over the fact that I had given out all the books she had packed. "We're going to have to order more," she noted as she shook her head at the dwindling stack.

"I suppose," I said. She always managed to keep a good supply on hand, and I never questioned when or how many she should order as long as we had enough to take with us. I was just getting ready to leave when Val came in wide-eyed and breathless.

"Karen just quit!" she announced.

Maria and I both began talking at once: "She quit?" "Are you sure?" "What happened?"

"I don't know," Val answered. "I heard her and Warde fighting, and then Phyllis joined in, then Karen came out of the bedroom and used the phone in my office to call a cab."

I picked up my purse and headed for the stairs. I found Karen on the front porch.

"What's going on? Val said you quit."

"I did. I've had it up to here!" she said, raising her hand to her forehead.

"Well, let me drive you home."

"I've already ordered a cab."

Karen was single-minded, and when she set her mind to something, there was no point in arguing. "At least tell me what happened."

Just then the cab pulled through the wrought-iron gates. Karen picked up her suitcase. "Tell Phyllis I'll get her suitcase back to her," she said as she jerked opened the cab door.

I couldn't imagine what the fight had been about. Nothing outstandingly bad had occurred during the week—just the usual irritations. I'd call Karen at home that night, or better yet, the next day. I hoped it was just temporary.

For the next couple of days the atmosphere in the house was strained. No one wanted to bring up Karen's leaving, but several times Maria and Val asked if I'd talked to her. I called her several times but got no answer. On the weekend, I drove over to her apartment in Hollywood. She opened the door almost as soon as I knocked. "Hi," she said, but her voice was icy, and for a moment I thought she might be mad at me. She waved me in.

"What's going on?"

"You don't know?"

"No. Everyone at the house is pussyfooting around, afraid to say anything. Val says you had a fight with Warde."

Karen plumped the cushions on her couch, punching each one thoroughly before she set it back in place.

"He wanted me to give him a permanent. At four in the afternoon, after eight days on the road, after getting up at the crack of dawn to get to the airport, and after sitting in a plane for five hours, he wants me to run down to the drugstore and come home and give him a Toni!" She punched the final cushion viciously.

I couldn't think of a thing to say. Whatever I said would only make it worse. I still hoped she would cool down and agree to come back to work.

I tried an oblique approach. "What are you going to do now?"

"I've already got another job."

"What?"

"And I'm going to be earning decent money for a change."

I'd made inquiries here and there, and discovered that the low salary Phyllis paid was about the norm in show business. Working for a celebrity was no way to get rich. I knew that Karen would be better off in a lot of ways if she left, but I couldn't imagine a more amiable or capable traveling companion, and it looked as if Phyllis would be going on the road again soon.

"It's not just the perm, Robin," she added after a few minutes of silence. "It's the whole thing. Being treated like a piece of furniture, never having time to yourself, having to do constant errands and menial tasks without so much as a 'thank you.' I guess I've just let them take me for granted too long and now I'm done."

Her mind was made up and I had to accept it. Phyllis did finally call Karen, even going so far as to offer more money, but Karen had closed that door.

22

I hated the first trip after Karen left. Phyllis had two appearances back-to-back in Texas: one at the Sunflower Festival in El Paso, and the next night, New Year's Eve, a concert appearance with the Dallas Symphony.

We left L.A. the morning of the Sunflower Festival and arrived in El Paso shortly after noon, in plenty of time for her appearance at dinner. We didn't even stay overnight but caught a late plane immediately after the show.

We didn't have a minute to spare between the end of the show and the time the plane left. Phyllis came offstage, stepped out of her costume and in one nearly continuous motion pulled on the white outfit I'd laid out. I dropped the dress, shoes, and gloves into the suitcase and zipped it shut while Phyllis put her wig into the wig box. One quick look around the dressing room to make sure we'd left nothing, and we were out of there.

The limousine driver had been watching for us and stashed the bags in the trunk. By the time he got behind the wheel, Phyllis, Warde, and I were settled inside.

We got to the plane by the skin of our teeth and clambered up the steps. The steward in the doorway took our boarding passes.

"I was afraid we weren't going to make it," I said.

In true Southern-hospitality fashion he said, "Oh, we'd always hold the plane for Miss Diller."

I could have slapped him.

Warde, who was just behind me, made a harrumphing noise that I knew meant something like "See? We didn't have to rush after all."

Of course, this was more than enough to justify his "I don't want to spend my precious time sitting around the airport" attitude. If Warde had been difficult before that, he was almost impossible afterward. He was convinced that any airline anywhere would hold a plane if Madam so desired.

Phyllis's appearance with the Dallas Symphony for its New Year's Eve Gala the next night was a major social event, and when Texans had social events, they did it up right.

When we checked into the Dallas Fairmont, the desk clerk handed me a stack of messages. One was from Ken, the publicist for the symphony. Even though it was late, I called him as soon as I got to my room.

"Will Phyllis do an interview after the rehearsal tomorrow?" he asked.

"I'm afraid not," I said. "Phyllis will do an interview to advertise an appearance, but this is already sold out, isn't it?"

"Yes."

"Well, there's no point then. People who hear the interview won't be able to get tickets, so no."

"Okay," he replied. *Boy, that was easy!* I had been prepared to be firm and even a little rude, if necessary, but he took the refusal with good grace. Then he said, "There's something else I want to ask."

"Okay."

"The Dallas Symphony Orchestra Guild wants to meet

Phyllis after the rehearsal. They have a special gift for her that can only be presented in person."

"I'll run it by Phyllis and let you know in the morning."

I woke up bright and early New Year's Eve morning and did a quick run-through of all the things I needed to do. I hoped that Phyllis hadn't stayed up late drinking with Warde. If so, she'd sleep until the last possible minute, and the only chance I'd have to ask about meeting with the guild would be in the limo on the way to rehearsal.

I ordered breakfast from room service before I took my shower. Ordinarily, I would have plenty of time to bathe and dress before the food arrived. I had not counted on the efficiency of the Dallas Fairmont. The breakfast arrived while I was still wrapped in a towel trying to make my recently cut hair do something other than lie on my head like a dead tarantula. The waiter's knock coincided with a knock on the door from the adjoining room. (The hotel had put us in a two-bedroom suite with our bedrooms separated by a luxurious living room.) At that particular moment the phone began to ring. New Year's Eve was going to be one of those days.

I yelled, "Just a moment," to whoever was knocking on whatever door, lurched for my bathrobe, snatched up the phone, and without even waiting to identify the caller, snapped, "Hold on," and dropped the receiver on the bed, then made my way to the door, avoiding the wet towel lying at my feet. Room service first.

While the waiter set up the table and got out the food, I unlocked the adjoining door to the suite. Surprisingly, it was Warde. Surprising because he was usually nursing a hangover at that time of day and was seldom out of bed before noon.

"Madam wants to know what time rehearsal is."

I swallowed the desire to tell him that it hadn't

changed from when she asked me last night. Instead I said, "It's at noon and I need to talk to Phyllis before we leave." I closed the door in his face, locked it, tipped the waiter and grabbed the phone receiver, which still lay on the bed.

"I wondered if you'd had a chance to talk to Miss Diller yet?" Ken, the publicist.

I bit back the urge to snarl at him and instead told him I'd call as soon as I had an answer and hung up. My stomach had signaled that I had better appease it and soon, and my hair was slowly drying into an unmanageable mop. That was when I realized I hadn't packed my curling iron.

By the time I finished breakfast and coaxed my hair into some semblance of order—with the aid of half a can of hair spray—I could hear the sound of a Bach étude from the living room next door. (The suite had a grand piano, which Phyllis required for practice.) I dressed and nearly swallowed my tongue when I went into the living room to find Phyllis dressed and evidently ready to get on with the day. We still had half an hour. Remarkable! Best of all, Warde was nowhere in sight, and I could put the proposition of meeting with the ladies' guild without him standing there saying, "Oh, Ada, you don't want to do that," as he inevitably would.

I told her that they wanted to meet with her for "just a few minutes" after the rehearsal and give her a present. She agreed but told me I would have to make it clear that it wasn't going to be a prolonged session.

"I don't want to be rushed tonight. I want time to come back here and rest before the concert. And find out what the present is," she added. "I don't want to be surprised." She turned back to the piano.

I called Ken. "Thank goodness," he said. "These ladies have been counting on meeting Miss Diller. They would not be happy if she refused."

"But no surprises," I said. "Phyllis wants to know what they're going to present her with."

He hesitated.

"I'll make it easy for you," I continued. "If you don't tell me, the meeting's off."

"It's a puppy," he said in a low voice, as if he didn't want the ladies to know he'd given up the surprise. Although surely they weren't all standing in his office. I hoped.

"A puppy?" I shrieked. I couldn't imagine a more unlikely present. "What kind of puppy?" Maybe it was a stuffed toy—a souvenir of her stay in Dallas.

"It's a purebred Lhasa Apso. One of the women breeds them," he explained. "This last litter she named in Phyllis's honor. All the dogs have names that start with *Ph*. There's Phancey, Phunney Phace, and Phearless. They want to give Phearless to Phyllis.

"A dog. You are talking about a real, live dog, right?"

"Yes. It's just a puppy."

"And it'll grow up to be a dog, right?"

"I guess so."

Wait'll I tell Phyllis they want to give her a dog. "I'll call you back."

In the living room, Phyllis was still practicing the Bach étude. I knew better than to interrupt, so I seated myself on the couch, where she could see me.

"Well?" she asked as she finished.

"It's a dog."

"What's a dog?"

"The present. They want to give you a puppy. A purebred Lhasa Apso, and they named it in honor of you."

"A puppy named Phyllis?"

"No, the puppy's name is Phearless." I explained the whole naming rigmarole to her.

"How delightful!"

I couldn't anticipate which way she would jump and was relieved that I didn't have to call Ken back and tell him no dog.

"Warde, listen to this," Phyllis said as Warde strolled into the room, towel-drying his newly permed hair. (Val had done it the day after Karen quit.)

"Tell him," Phyllis instructed, so I repeated the story for Warde.

"That's wonderful, honey," he said. "Just think, it'll be a companion for Candy."

I sat there stunned. I would never have predicted that either Phyllis or Warde would be happy about getting another dog. And I doubted that Candy—a cute little Bichon Frise that received 100 percent of the attention from 100 percent of the people in the house—felt the need for a companion. Still, I couldn't help but picture what a charming pair they'd make—two mop dogs.

On the way to the rehearsal, Phyllis had one instruction about the dog: "They are going to keep it overnight. Tell them they can bring it to the plane in the morning."

Thank heaven! I really didn't want to spend New Year's Eve baby-sitting a homesick pup.

"I'll tell them," I promised.

The rehearsal went about the same as usual. Once I had everything set up in the dressing room, I stepped into the wings, where I could hear snatches of music followed by laughter. Phyllis loved to clown, and when the members of the orchestra found that she really could play, they were happy to accept Phyllis as one of them and pleased to be entertained along the way. If Phyllis didn't get through the entire number without a few mistakes, well, what difference would that make? The audience would be expecting a comedy routine anyway.

Toward the end of the rehearsal, I slipped back to the

dressing room, astonished to find Ken already there with a dozen ladies. Ken had met us as soon as we arrived and it never occurred to me that we should discuss the way the meeting was going to happen. This would not do at all. Phyllis would want to come back and catch her breath, maybe use the bathroom and relax a few minutes before meeting with the ladies of the guild. Ken introduced me, and I was by then getting used to being considered something of a celebrity myself—all because I worked for a "star."

I made all the right noises about how much Phyllis was looking forward to meeting them and how pleased she was that the proceeds of that night's gala were going to charity. (I had noticed that on a poster outside.) Then I made a quick motion to Ken, and he stepped outside for a conference in the hall.

"They can't be in here when Phyllis comes offstage," I whispered. "You're going to have to get them out for a few minutes."

It seemed to me a touchy situation, but Ken handled it smoothly, ushering the ladies into a vacant dressing room next door so that "Miss Diller can have a little privacy before we all descend on her." There was much good-natured, Southern-belle giggling and that was that.

Once rehearsal ended and Phyllis had a few minutes to relax, I popped next door to give Ken the thumbs up. As always, Phyllis was gracious, and the ladies of the Dallas Symphony Orchestra Guild were "enchanted" to meet her. The presentation of Phearless went without a hitch, and I was surprised to see how small the dog was. She sat demurely in her breeder's cupped hands while everyone reached out to touch her and remark on her resemblance to Phyllis.

They both did have shaggy hair.

The president of the guild told Phyllis that after the

concert she was having a New Year's Eve party, "and of course you're invited. You and your charming husband. After all, it's New Year's Eve in Dallas, and we want to show you some of our true Texas hospitality."

Phyllis muttered something noncommittal and I knew she'd want to check with Warde.

The performance that evening went as smoothly as Phyllis's concerts usually did. That is to say, there were a lot of ad libs and unrehearsed interruptions. As always, she was billed as *Dame Illya Dillya*, and she appeared onstage in that gorgeous opera coat and long white gloves (the same white gloves Karen had stitched the yard of material onto in Pittsburgh for the Little Old Lady skit). She wore a glittering tiara in her fright wig, which gave a wonderfully comic effect. After the applause died down, she began removing the gloves with a sophisticated smile. As she kept pulling and the glove kept getting longer, she'd cast somewhat anxious "stay with me" glances at the audience. Then, as the glove continued to "grow," she actually began to look embarrassed and try to hide her hands by half turning around.

By the time the gloves were truly and finally removed, the audience was in stitches. The magnificent blue opera coat, which was lined with white satin and glittered with crystals, came next. She took it off to reveal a gorgeous white satin gown cut moderately low in front and even lower in back.

Following her "strip," Phyllis seated herself at the piano with a look of apprehension, mugging at the conductor and the audience. Finally, the concert began and the people in the audience sat in amazement, staring intently as Phyllis Diller actually played the piano. Bach and Chopin rippled from her fingers, and when she finished, the audience went wild with applause and enthusiasm. Perhaps because it was New Year's Eve, people were in a particularly jovial mood. The concert ended with a standing ovation.

Afterward, well-wishers flooded Phyllis's dressing room. Part of my job was to keep everyone outside until she had changed and had a few minutes to herself. Warde mixed drinks while I helped her out of the long, white gown and folded it neatly into the suitcase. By the time Phyllis had put on a party dress, I had everything packed and ready to be taken out to the limo. All that remained was to make sure we had all the music.

Each orchestra librarian collected the music after the performance, and I touched base with him (or her) during the rehearsal to make sure ours would be put back into our music bag. While Phyllis and Warde were busy hobnobbing in the dressing room with the crème de la crème of Dallas society, I went in search of the librarian. Sure enough, our music had been neatly packed in our music bag, and I went through it to make sure every part was there. It cost a small fortune to have the musical arrangements written out for each instrument, and losing any of it would be expensive. I didn't want that happening on my watch.

When I'd seen the music bag, along with the costume case and wig box, safely stowed in the back of the limo, I returned to the dressing room. The last of the well-wishers was leaving, and I gave the room a final check to make sure nothing had been left behind.

"Is the music taken care of?" Phyllis asked as I closed the door to the closet.

"Yes, everything's in the car."

Ken poked his head in. "You're coming to the party?"

"We're just going to drop Robin off at the hotel with the bags and then we'll be right along."

"Oh, no, Robin's invited, too." Ken smiled for the first time since I'd met him that morning. Everything had gone smoothly and he'd finally relaxed.

Warde piped up. "No, she has to take the bags back to the hotel. It's her job."

I couldn't believe that I was going to be left alone in a hotel on New Year's Eve while everyone else went off to a party. I looked to Phyllis in appeal, but she was busying herself in front of the mirror. It was one of those times she chose not to get involved.

Ken looked at me and I shrugged. As we trooped out to the car he touched my arm and pulled me aside. "I'll come and get you in a few minutes."

I shook my head and hoped he couldn't see that I was blinking back tears. I knew that once again Warde was exercising his right to make decisions and demonstrating his "class." He didn't want a mere secretary at the same party as he.

As usual, I slid into the front seat of the limo with the driver, and if it seemed longer to get back to the hotel than it should have, no one seemed to notice. I simply assumed the driver was taking a different route until he pulled up in front of a grand, two-story, colonial-style house set back about half the length of a football field from the street. The front door stood open and we could see people milling around inside. In a flash, the hostess was beside the car.

"Here are the guests of honor!" she cried. "Come in, come in!" She opened my door the same time the chauffeur opened the back for Phyllis and Warde. The hostess took me by the arm and grabbed Phyllis with her other hand.

"Now the party will really get going!" she exclaimed as she propelled us toward the house. Warde trailed behind and I knew he was seething. The delicious idea of Warde throwing one of his temper tantrums flitted across my mind, but I didn't think he'd had enough to drink that he'd lose his self-control.

As soon as we were inside, a maid reached out to take our wraps.

"You did make it!" Ken was standing in the entrance hall holding a drink.

"Robin can't stay," Warde said as he divested himself of his mink. "She has things to do back at the hotel."

"Oh, surely for just one drink," the hostess urged. "After all, it is New Year's Eve."

But Warde turned his back on her and strutted after Phyllis, who was already being fawned over by excited guests.

"I'd better not," I said. "But thank you so much for including me. I really do appreciate it."

She gave me a hug and said, "I'm so sorry." However, it wasn't her battle and as long as Phyllis was there, that was the important thing.

I could have stayed but wouldn't have enjoyed myself knowing there would be a scene later and that Warde would go out of his way to make life miserable for me as long as he could. I waved good-bye to Ken and was relieved to find the limousine still parked in the driveway. I huddled in the back seat and sniffled all the way to the hotel.

Back at the Dallas Fairmont, I followed the bellman and our cart of bags to the room and tipped him outrageously. I considered going back down to the bar and having a drink by myself, but although it had looked quite cheerful when I'd passed, I'd never gone into a bar by myself and just couldn't bear to start that night.

Feeling utterly miserable, I took off the white-and-gold dress I'd worn for New Year's and turned on the television. *The King and I* was just beginning. Evidently someone down at the station knew that there would be a few people home alone on New Year's Eve.

After the movie, I crawled into bed and wondered

what I'd have been doing if Karen had been here. *Maybe I should quit, too.*

It was not a pleasant feeling on which to begin a new year.

23

The schedule for the coming year looked pretty hectic, and more dates were being added all the time. First up was a trip to Harrah's in Lake Tahoe.

Bill Harrah, who owned Harrah's Hotel and Casino in both Lake Tahoe and Reno, had a reputation for treating his stars like royalty. We flew from Los Angeles to Lake Tahoe in Bill Harrah's private jet and were met at the plane by a chocolate-brown Rolls Royce, which took us to the house on the lake where Phyllis and Warde would stay. The house had been stocked with plenty of food and their favorite brands of liquor. No need to bring Phyllis's kitchen bag or Warde's red leather "booze bag."

As the Rolls approached the house, I couldn't stop staring. It sat at the edge of the lake and the sun sparkled off the snow, which covered the beach. The chauffeur parked under the *porte cochère*, opened the door, and ushered us inside.

"Wow!" I said, and Phyllis said, "Yeah!" We were standing in the living room, which was nearly all glass and had a huge rock fireplace on one side. Outside were wooden decks that overlooked Lake Tahoe.

While we took it all in, the chauffeur brought in the

luggage. "Master bedroom's in here," he said as he headed toward the back of the house. I checked to see that the suitcases were actually for the house and not the dressing room, then checked out the kitchen—large enough to hold a party. I went back out with the chauffeur and pointed out the costume bags and wig boxes to be delivered to the dressing room.

"That's Miss Diller's car for her to use," he said, nodding to a sleek, black Chrysler. He handed me the keys. "The Rolls will come pick them up whenever they call for it."

Once we got all the bags in the house, I told Phyllis I'd go check into my room and gave her the keys for the Chrysler. Perry was coming up for a couple of days to go skiing, and Phyllis was delighted. When she was away so much, she really didn't have time to spend with her family. That pleased me, too, because it meant Phyllis would be occupied and I'd have more time to myself.

For some reason there was no hotel room for me—perhaps the Harrah's people thought I would be staying at the house. I ended up at the motel next door to Harrah's. It meant a walk across the dark, snow-covered parking lot in the freezing cold late at night, but I still preferred that to staying at the house with the family.

Phyllis had not yet replaced Karen and considered doing away with a dresser entirely. While she thought it over, I inherited some of Karen's duties. One of them was the hand warmer Phyllis used at the end of her stand-up routine before she sat down to play the piano. Roy had convinced Phyllis to play the piano at the end of her act. After all, he reasoned, she had practiced for the symphonies, and it was something different that people would not be expecting. She agreed to give it a try.

The hand warmer consisted of a small metal case that had porous, nonflammable material inside and was filled with lighter fluid. Once it was lit and the lid back on, I'd slip the little case into a flannel drawstring bag. It was a cute little gizmo, and I supposed skiers and hikers would use it outdoors in snow country.

It was my first experience with the thing. Karen had always filled the hand warmer just before each performance and set it on the edge of the piano, along with a glass of water and a small box of tissues. The first few nights went smoothly enough, and I congratulated myself on getting into the routine. Until one night when I got into real trouble.

Phyllis was in the inner dressing room, Warde was out in the hallway, and I was sitting at a little coffee table filling the hand warmer. I always had to remember to buy lighter fluid for the pesky thing—we seemed to go through it so fast. I'd overestimated the amount of fluid and before I knew it, the hand warmer overflowed. Lighter fluid dribbled down the sides and ran onto the table.

What a mess!

I grabbed a nearby towel and mopped it up, surprised to find how much I'd spilled. One end of the towel was damp. I dropped it on the floor as I got up to wash my hands at the wet bar. While there, I got the glass of ice water ready. I used plenty of ice because it would sit on the piano under the hot lights. By the time Phyllis was ready for it at the end of her monologue, the ice would have melted, leaving her a glass of cool water.

On my way back to the couch, I stopped by the big, red bowl of potato chips on the bar. I broke a few chips in half, as I'd seen Karen do. Phyllis never felt as guilty if she just ate the broken ones. Karen always made sure that there were some for her to find. We joked that the calories escaped when the chips were broken.

My last chore before we trooped upstairs to the stage was to light the hand warmer. It burned for forty-five minutes, and if I lit it too soon, or hadn't filled it quite full, it would go out by the time Phyllis reached for it.

I set the glass of ice water on the edge of the coffee table and picked up the book of matches. As soon as I touched the match to the material inside the hand warmer, flames leapt up and ran down the side where the fluid had spilled. Instinctively, I dropped it and watched in horror as the fluid ran out and little blue flames flashed over the table top.

"Warde!" I screamed. "Warde! Help! FIRE!" I desperately groped for something to put out the fire. The towel, my first thought, was damp with flammable liquid, which I mercifully realized before I tried to use it to smother the flames. My pulse started to race as I watched flames cover the entire table top.

No one had come in response to my scream—the band upstairs was in full swing and the downstairs speakers were turned all the way up. It was almost impossible to carry on a normal conversation and obviously no one had heard me. I was terribly frightened and had visions of the flames spreading onto the rug and catching the entire dressing room on fire with Phyllis and me trapped inside.

Some instinct made me reach behind and grab one of the sofa cushions. I emptied the glass of water onto it and fighting the urge to run, pressed the cushion on the table top. When I picked it up, the flames had lessened. I repeated that several times and suddenly it was all over. The little blue tongues of flame were gone; the sofa cushion was soggy and warm.

My pulse continued to race and my knees shook so badly that I collapsed onto the couch. Gingerly, I reached out to touch the hand warmer and jerked my hand away. It was blistering hot. Using a fresh towel, I managed to fit the top on and maneuvered it into the drawstring bag.

Just then Warde came strolling in.

"What do I smell?" he asked.

"Lighter fluid." I nodded toward the hand warmer.

"Oh. Is Madam ready?"

Phyllis emerged from the inner dressing room.

"Are we all ready?" she chirped.

I nodded dumbly. With the immediate crisis over, shock began to set in. I didn't want to talk. I didn't want to move.

"What's this towel doing on the floor?" Warde asked as he almost tripped over it.

"Have you got everything?" Phyllis asked as she headed for the door.

"I need to get your water," I said and picked up the empty glass.

"Well, hurry up," Phyllis said. "You should have had that all ready." Apparently she hadn't smelled the lighter fluid.

My hands were shaking as I dropped the ice cubes in. Warde and Phyllis were already on their way upstairs by the time I closed the door and followed them. As I walked down the hall, I noticed the fire extinguisher on the wall. Never again would I be so foolish as to not note their locations when we checked into a hotel or settled into a dressing room.

24

Phyllis's next engagement was in Las Vegas, once again at the Riviera. John Davidson's contract had expired and Phyllis would have a new opening act. Roy suggested a singer by the name of Barbara McNair. At that time, she was appearing at the Coconut Grove in Los Angeles. Back in the '30s, the Coconut Grove had been the "in" place in L.A.—a large, elegant nightclub set in the acres of lush grounds of the Ambassador Hotel, surrounded by graceful palm trees and semitropical plants. Sammy Davis Jr. had recently purchased it, renamed it "The Now Grove," and was trying to make it the "in" place once again.

"Would you like to go to The Grove with us?" Phyllis asked one afternoon. "Roy has a singer he wants me to consider as my opening act."

"Sure. Sounds like fun." I had memories of the Coconut Grove from my high school prom. I wondered how it would be a dozen years later. I found it every bit as elegant as it had been then, and I hoped it would get the patronage it deserved.

My gosh. Barbara McNair was gorgeous! She reminded me a bit of Diahann Carroll. Her voice was powerful but sweet. After the performance, we adjourned to the dressing room with a lot of other people. Outside of Phyllis and Warde, there were Roy and Phyllis's William Morris agent, Mr. Moch, along with Barbara McNair's agent, Barbara's boyfriend, and two other men who were never introduced.

If Barbara was gorgeous onstage, up close she was stunning. She wore a silky robe and very little makeup and was still beautiful. I suddenly realized I was staring and managed to drag my eyes away. *They're going to think I'm queer for her if I don't stop staring,* I told myself, and I wondered if anyone else was as struck by her beauty as I was.

Whatever they felt, everyone agreed that Barbara would be Phyllis's opening act at the Riviera in Las Vegas, scheduled for the first two weeks in February.

February in Las Vegas is too cold to sit by the pool, so I had little to do except handle correspondence. Phyllis and Warde stayed at their house, and I had a room at the hotel. I was free during the day and only met them backstage just before show time. Phyllis and I spent the break between shows going over correspondence. I spent a lot of my day typing letters and even went so far as to write replies to fan letters for her. As a rule, fan letters received a stock reply, if any at all, but I enjoyed doing something different, and Phyllis appreciated her fans. Having a personal reply from her would make someone's day. I would give them to Phyllis backstage, and she'd sign them for me to mail.

Phyllis changed her show somewhat. At the end, instead of doing her piano number, she invited Barbara to come onstage and they sang a song together. In fact, the song they sang was titled *Together*. It was a fascinating contrast: Barbara was tall, black and willowy, wearing an elegant, black sheath of utter simplicity. Phyllis was shorter, covered in glittering sequins, and had hair that looked like she had just stuck her finger in an electric socket.

At rehearsals everything went well and the two women established a rapport that added sparkle to their performance. Barbara's pianist and road manager, Perk, had an easy way of keeping things moving with a light touch and sense of humor. It would be a great combination. He kidded with Phyllis and Barbara and made everything seem fun while he showed them how to work together.

The dressing rooms were side by side, with the wardrobe room at the end of the hall. Sometimes when Phyllis was onstage, I sat in the wardrobe room with Margie, the old woman who had been the wardrobe mistress at the Riviera for as long as anyone could remember, and watched as she methodically stitched and repaired costumes.

"That Barbara," she said to me one night. "I don't know 'bout her." Disapproval dripped from her voice.

"Why not, Margie?" I couldn't imagine that gorgeous creature with the winning smile and shy manner doing anything that would upset anyone.

"Do you know what she wears under that dress of hers?" Margie paused mid-stitch to fix me with a baleful glare. "Not a thing! Not a stitch of clothing!"

I couldn't tell if her tone of voice conveyed disgust or awe. "What would happen, I ask you, just what would happen if one of those little straps was to break? She'd be standing there on that stage in front of hundreds of people absolutely stark naked." She paused to consider this. "With the spotlight on her," she added under her breath.

I had to bite back a laugh. I wondered if Margie was as scandalized as she acted. Truly, the chances of a strap breaking while Barbara was onstage seemed remote. I chuckled at Margie's assumed outrage, however, and wondered if she secretly hoped that would happen. It never did.

25

Shortly after we arrived in Vegas, some friends of Warde's from the East came for a visit. They stayed at the house with Phyllis and Warde, which did not please Phyllis. It ate away at the little privacy she had, and while she tried to be the gracious hostess, I could tell her patience was wearing thin. She became short-tempered with me and Warde, and he wisely removed himself from her periphery whenever possible. Of course, I didn't have that option.

The third night into the engagement Warde chose to take his friends out for dinner in high style. They had already seen Phyllis's first show from the choice booth the hotel kept for VIPs, then Warde took them to dinner at Caesars Palace.

When the stage manager, Bob, called "fifteen minutes," Warde still hadn't returned. Because of the complex rehearsals, no one had found time to put Warde's announcement on tape. Warde almost always did the announcements for Phyllis. She had asked him to record it "just in case," and he assured her he would, but so far he hadn't.

It was a pity in more ways than one. When Warde had done the announcement the first night, he introduced

Phyllis as "the star of the show." The contract had been explicit that Phyllis and Barbara shared equal billing. When Perk objected to Warde's announcement, Warde agreed to stick to the phrasing, "the *comedy* star of the show." However, the previous night he had once again left out the word "comedy" during the announcement for both shows, and there had been phone calls from Barbara's agent to Phyllis's, warning Phyllis that it would have to stop. Phyllis wanted to get the announcement on tape in order to prevent Warde from perpetrating his mischief any further and before relations started to deteriorate.

At that particular moment, I knew that Phyllis wished that she had insisted on Warde recording it. The show was about to start, which meant about forty-five minutes before she went onstage.

"Call Caesars' gourmet room," she instructed me, "and tell them to come back at once."

I called Caesars and finally got Warde on the phone. Phyllis reached out and took the receiver from me. "Warde? Warde, where are you? The show is about to start. I need you here." She sounded calm, but I could sense the exasperation in her voice. "Well, I'm going to send Robin to pick you up. Just be outside."

There was some muttering on the other end, and I assumed he was whining about having to come back when they were having such a good time.

"Now, Warde!" Phyllis barked and hung up.

Barbara's act took thirty-five minutes, so I had just enough time to get to Caesars and back before Phyllis went onstage. As I tore out the stage door, I could hear the orchestra playing Barbara's opening number.

Caesars Palace was quite a way from the Riviera, and I was glad that it wasn't a weekend night when there'd be traffic. Phyllis had phoned the Riviera valet from the dressing room and told them to get her car out front. They were pulling it up just as I raced through the door.

I took Paradise, a back road, as far as I could. When I turned onto the Strip, I hit one red light after another. Thank heaven Warde and his friends were out front when I arrived. I leaned over and opened the passenger door, but Warde came around and motioned me to move over. He was drunk and in no condition to be behind the wheel. What should I do? Get out and take a cab back to the Riviera?

No, I did what I always did; I caved.

I scooted over and held my breath for the wild ride back at top speed. Warde liked to fantasize that he was a race car driver. He would lower the seat back as far as it would go so he was nearly lying down because that's how race car drivers did it. He could barely see over the steering wheel. By God's grace we arrived without actually having an accident, and I found myself shaking when my foot touched the blessed ground in front of the Riviera.

"What time is it?" I asked Warde.

He didn't answer, but one of his friends said, "Twelve twenty-two." We'd made remarkable time.

I thanked him and headed through the casino for the stage door. As I reached it, I realized that Warde was not behind me. I glanced back to see him standing by the craps table with his friends. Clearly, he wasn't going to let them see him being ordered around.

I continued backstage, surprised to find Phyllis standing in the wings, ten minutes early.

"Where is he?" Any pretense of patience had gone.

"He stopped to play craps."

"Damn!" For a lady who didn't swear, that signaled big trouble. "Go get him!"

I just stood there and she glared at me, then she shrugged. "You're right—it wouldn't do any good."

"He'll be here in a moment," I offered. It was the wrong thing to say. She was already mad and now she was mad at me!

"What do you know about it?" she snarled with cold fury. "He'll be here when he gets damn good and ready. Damn!" She began to pace. "We can't wait," she said a moment later. We both looked at the big clock in Bob's office. 12:30. "Come on," she said, then grabbed me by the elbow and marched into the office.

"Bob, I need a large piece of paper and a marker." Bob slid them both across his desk with alacrity.

"I want you to write the announcement," she told me, "then get it out to Perk as soon as the curtain comes down."

Perk had a mike on his piano, and as the curtain fell at the end of Barbara's show he would say, "Barbara McNair, ladies and gentlemen. Barbara McNair." He would then switch off the mike and leave the stage as the orchestra began a drum roll and Warde, at the offstage mike, would make Phyllis's announcement, which she was dictating to me in Bob's office: "And now, ladies and gentlemen (pause), the comedy star of our show (pause), PHYLLIS DILLER!"

Although my printing would not win any prizes, it was legible and it was large. The only problem was to make Perk aware of what was going on.

We hurried into the wings and Phyllis whispered to me, "As soon as the curtain comes down, run out and hand this to Perk before he switches his mike off. Don't forget, it's live—you can't say anything to him."

Barbara McNair was into her last number, and Phyllis and I stood anxiously just out of sight of the audience, trying to get Perk's attention. Fortunately, he was facing us and just as Barbara swung into her finale, he glanced our way. I began making frantic motions for him to stay put, not to leave the stage. He looked puzzled and shook his head slightly. He had no idea what I was trying to tell him.

"As soon as the curtain hits the stage," Phyllis said again. "If you go out earlier, the audience will be able to see your feet."

Barbara began taking her bows and Perk led her play-off music. I heard the massive curtain starting to rattle down from twenty feet above us. I glanced at it, then out at Perk, who was doing his "Barbara McNair, ladies and gentlemen" bit.

"The curtain!" Phyllis yelled in my ear over the blaring orchestra. "Watch the curtain!" She screamed so loud I was certain the people in the front row heard her. It was only a few inches above my head and dropping fast. I was ready to run when suddenly she hit me so hard that I lost my balance and I staggered backward. "The *curtain!*" she shrieked.

The bottom of the curtain hit the floor with a solid "thunk." I had been standing directly beneath it. Fortunately, I didn't have a moment to consider what would have happened if Phyllis hadn't shoved me out of the way. I could see Perk reaching for his mike.

Phyllis said, "Go!" and I dashed out onstage.

"Read this," I mouthed as I thrust the paper into his hand. He looked at me in puzzlement. "Now!" I whispered urgently, pointing to the microphone on the piano. Phyllis stood just offstage, nodding vigorously.

He glanced once more from me to Phyllis to the paper, then he dived in. Clearing his throat slightly, he pulled the mike closer and read: "Ladies and Gentlemen, pause, the Riviera Hotel is proud to present the comedy star of our show, pause, Phyllis Diller."

As he read the first "pause" out loud, I whirled around in horror. I started to signal him, but he was already onto the second one, and I couldn't do anything about it. By the time he finished, Phyllis was onstage, telling her first joke.

I stopped in the wings just offstage, and Perk walked by me muttering, "I don't believe I did that. I really don't believe I did that."

I started to laugh and couldn't stop. I stumbled into Bob's office and collapsed into a chair, gasping for breath.

A moment later Warde wandered in. "Where's Phyllis?" he asked, looking around as if we might be hiding her somewhere. I was still gasping and couldn't answer. Bob just looked at him with the disdain he reserved for the HOTS (Husbands Of The Stars), as he called them. "She's onstage, Warde."

"Oh." Warde turned and sauntered back out the stage door.

"You could've been killed tonight," Bob said as he watched Warde disappear. "Do you know how much that curtain weighs?"

"Don't tell me," I begged when I finally caught my breath. "I heard what it sounded like when it hit."

"Yeah, because the bottom is lined with a quarter ton of lead weights."

I stared at him for a moment as his words sank in. "It's really been an awful night."

"Tell you what," he said and sat back in his chair. "When the show's over, I'll buy you a drink."

"Make it a martini." It would be only the second martini I'd ever had, but that night I figured I deserved it, and I definitely needed it.

As soon as Phyllis changed out of her costume and we closed up the dressing room, I headed for the bar. Bob was already there with a tall drink in front of him.

"Ah, here you are. Ready for that martini?" He smiled and I realized he really did have beautiful gray eyes.

I slid onto the bar stool next to him. "I've changed my mind. I'll have a glass of white wine."

"Pantywaist."

"Yeah, that's me."

The bartender stepped over, and Bob ordered the wine and another drink for himself, then turned to me. "So, do you like off-roading?" he asked.

"Uh, off-what?"

"Really? You've never taken a Jeep out in the desert? Up in the mountains? Off the roads?"

Such a thing had never occurred to me.

The bartender set our drinks down and Bob finished off the old one in a quick gulp. "There is a beautiful little spring back in the mountains," he said. "The water is ice cold. Wanna go?"

"What? Now?"

"Why not?"

I wasn't at all sure I wanted to go to an ice-cold spring up in the mountains in the middle of a winter night. I am not adventurous and this seemed bizarre. Bob, I came to find out, loved the night. He came alive a couple of hours after sunset.

"So?" he said.

Okay, what else have I got to do? Watch television until I get sleepy? Read a mystery? Why not, indeed?

"Yeah, okay. Why not?"

Bob signaled the bartender for a couple of more drinks. "To go," he said.

With our drinks in Styrofoam "go cups," we made a quick exit through the back of the casino.

"Here we are." Bob opened the door of his Jeep and I hopped in. Thank goodness he kept a couple of down jackets in the back.

"Put this on," he said, tossing me one. "It's cold out there."

We were away from the neon in almost no time, and I looked up through the open top of the Jeep at millions of stars. The night was incredibly dark and, wow, cold! He hadn't been just a-woofin'.

"Here it is," he said about forty minutes later. We had left the pavement and were bumping along a dirt track. Even in the dark, I could tell it was not a real road. Bushes and weeds brushed against the sides.

We clambered out of the Jeep—thank heaven I'd worn slacks that night—and I could hear falling water nearby. Bob put his arm around me and guided me a few feet to a lovely little spring that sparkled under the stars. We both knelt down and drank—the water was ice cold, just as he'd promised.

Somewhere nearby a dog started barking.

"Coyote," Bob said.

I was back in the Jeep in five seconds.

Bob laughed at me. "It's just a wild dog. It won't hurt you."

"Not as long as I'm in the Jeep it won't."

The ride back into town was like night and day—literally. Coming out to the spring, the lights had been behind us and all I could see was the sky full of stars and the dark, towering mountains. On the way back, the view was all neon and bright lights.

The next day I slept until noon.

The rest of the engagement was as smooth as could be. Warde recorded his announcement so he was free to go and play with his friends, but once he'd done it, he seemed to want to be with Phyllis all the time. I was sure they'd had it out and he knew he was on very thin ice. Phyllis and I didn't work much, and I found myself spending more time with Bob at the little bar just outside the stage door where the crew and orchestra gathered for drinks after the show.

Sometimes Bob and I talked until nearly sunrise. It

didn't matter how late I stayed up—I could sleep all day if I wanted to. It was turning into a pretty laid-back gig.

Because Phyllis didn't do a lot of work during this time, I was in and out of the dressing room just long enough to make sure she had everything she needed. Sometimes, during Barbara's numbers, we'd run through the mail quickly. With Warde hanging around being smarmy as hell, I got out of there as soon as I could. Whenever possible I'd go downstairs to listen to Barbara and watch her onstage.

One night I asked Phyllis, "Why is it I've never heard of her before?" I'd been around a bit since the day when I hadn't heard of Totie Fields and felt that by then I was at least acquainted with most of the names in our end of show business.

"She's got a problem," Phyllis said.

I knew it couldn't be drugs. Phyllis was death on drugs, and I was sure she would never knowingly consent to work with someone who indulged in that poison.

"What kind of problem?"

"You've seen her boyfriend?" she asked as she fished distractedly through the bowl of potato chips.

"The short, not very attractive man who's always hanging around? That's her boyfriend?"

"That's the one."

I frowned. They were definitely not a matched pair. "What about him?" I asked, hoping she'd fill me in before Warde got back from wherever he'd disappeared to.

"Well, he can't fly and he won't let her travel alone, so she has to take the train everywhere. Or they drive. You know that can kill a road trip."

I thought of our upcoming two-month, nonstop tour that would take us from the West Coast to the East, down to Puerto Rico and back to Chicago, all in one grueling circuit. "Why can't he fly? Does he have a phobia?"

"He carries a gun."

I stared at her for a moment. "A gun? Why does he carry a gun?"

Phyllis looked at me as if I were being purposely obtuse. She had been dancing around the question for several minutes and obviously was loath to come right out and say it.

"Why do you think he carries a gun?"

"Well, I don't think he's a cop. So, he's a . . ." I looked at Phyllis to finish the sentence.

She just nodded.

"He's a mobster?"

Phyllis shrugged but said nothing.

I slumped in my chair, stunned into silence. How could someone as lovely and so sweet get mixed up with someone like that? Maybe she wasn't as lovely and sweet as I'd thought. But there was no doubt she was stunningly gorgeous and a wonderful singer. What a shame. What a damned shame.

After we left Las Vegas, I watched for Barbara McNair's name in the trade papers, but she didn't appear often.

I felt a little sorry when we left the Riviera. I knew I'd miss Bob and some of the late-night adventures, like the lodge up at Mount Charleston, which was open twenty-four hours a day. I loved the lodge, with its circular fireplace. The first night Bob took me there, somebody had a guitar and the half-dozen people still there at 3:00 a.m. sang old folk songs. The night before we left, Bob took me there again. The moon was full and glittered on the snow—who would think that barely an hour out of the neon jungle we'd be in beautiful pine forests with waist-high snow? Yeah, I was going to miss Bob. On the other hand, I was glad to get away from Barbara McNair's group of creepy hangers-on who were always with her. I just hoped it all worked out for her.

26

After we returned from Las Vegas, we had one day in L.A. before leaving on the longest continuous trip I'd ever imagined. It was a nine-week, forty-suitcase trip, starting and ending in Chicago, with Georgia, New York, New Jersey, Puerto Rico, and Arkansas in between. It's not that we hadn't been on the road for long periods before, but nine weeks without coming home seemed like a marathon.

That first day we flew into Chicago, then drove a couple of hours to a cute little dinner theater called "Pheasant Run." The place was barely a wide spot in the road, with a motel at one end and the Pheasant Run Dinner Theater at the other. Connecting the two were a handful of "country stores" selling crafts and souvenirs, a dress shop that had some lovely things—including some outrageously priced bathing suits—a small deli, a sort of drugstore, and a restaurant. The motel had a swimming pool, both indoors and out—one could swim under a glass partition to get to the outside part.

Phyllis's youngest daughter, Stephanie, and Warde were doing a play together called *Forty Carats*. That was the first time I had seen Warde work other than the time he'd opened for Phyllis in Pittsburgh.

We stayed a few days—long enough for Phyllis to get her family settled into a big, old farmhouse she had rented a few miles away. Once again, I was thrilled that I would not be staying at the house with them—I had a cute little room at the Pheasant Run Inn. I went down to the theater and watched the rehearsals a couple of days, pleasantly surprised that both Warde and Stephanie seemed quite at home on the stage.

Opening night went swimmingly, the audience responded with much laughter and applause, and the cast was rewarded with several curtain calls. Everyone was in a good mood. The theater owner, Carl Stone, threw a party backstage, and I joined in for a bit, congratulating everyone involved. I'd expected Warde to be arrogant and condescending, but he was relaxed and gracious. For the first time I could see the man Phyllis had been attracted to and was touched by her absolute delight in his success. Perhaps once everyone could see he wasn't just "Mr. Phyllis Diller," he felt better about life.

Phyllis would have liked to have stayed at Pheasant Run a few more days and enjoy family time with her daughter, but she had places to go and shows to do.

The next day, the limo picked me up shortly after dawn. A brief detour took us to the farmhouse where Phyllis was waiting. The driver stuffed as many suitcases as possible into the trunk, and the rest shared the back seat with Phyllis. We arrived at O'Hare Airport in Chicago in plenty of time; Phyllis liked to be early. From Chicago we flew to Atlanta, where we changed to a private plane that took us to Albany, Georgia. Phyllis had a one-night appearance at the Chamber of Commerce banquet.

The pilot of the small plane stayed overnight in Albany and flew us back to Atlanta early in the morning. Two early-morning flights in a row, changing planes, rehearsal the day before, and a full day ahead of us had us both dragging. And, gee, this was just the beginning of our marathon. Thank goodness there was a passenger service representative to smooth the way as we headed for that 10:15 flight to New York. Phyllis's regular chauffeur, Jimmy Simpson, met us and I breathed a little easier. Jimmy knew exactly how Phyllis liked things done. Phyllis had a one-night stand the following night, and that afternoon she taped a couple of radio commercials. Radio, thank goodness, was nothing like television and took only a couple of hours. She had looked over the scripts on the plane.

"Won't they ever realize that one person can only say so much in thirty seconds?" She shook her head over the manuscript. "Look at this. The basic rule is one word a second. There must be fifty words there."

I counted them. "Forty-eight."

"Forty-eight words and how many laughs?"

"Three laughs."

"One laugh takes about three seconds. That's going to be tough."

We went directly to the hotel—my room was next to hers at the Plaza. We had just enough time to check in and get lunch from room service. The taping started at 3:00, and on the way to the studio, Phyllis rehearsed the scripts. It was a tribute to Jimmy's iron nerves that he didn't plow us into a fire hydrant. Phyllis's three-laughs-per-thirty-seconds in the enclosed confines of the car were positively riveting.

At the studio, Phyllis romped through the rehearsals. In spite of the forty-eight words and three laughs, she managed to get it all in clearly. One of Phyllis's favorite words was "precise." Her diction for these commercials would be "precise," she told me. And "crisp." She liked "crisp." She sailed right through the taping and finished up well before six o'clock.

"Phone Mr. B and tell him we're leaving for Sardi's," she told me as we were getting ready to leave the studio. Earlier she had talked with Mr. B, her attorney and business manager, and they had agreed to a dinner meeting.

Jimmy drove us to Sardi's, where I had already reserved a table. Warde wasn't with us, so I was included because Phyllis was never alone in a public place. Sardi's fascinated me—a true New York legend. It wasn't elaborate, but it had been the gathering place of show people for decades. I could hardly wait to write to my parents and to Ingrid and tell them all about it. When we were seated, I automatically grabbed the two books of matches in the ashtrays and pocketed them. I didn't smoke, but Ingrid had a matchbook collection and asked me to bring matches from wherever we went. Phyllis had even begun doing it, routinely gathering matchbooks from hotel rooms, restaurants, and dinner theaters for Ingrid's collection.

When Phyllis noticed me putting the matchbooks in my purse, she said, "I think we can do better than that." She summoned the waiter and explained what she wanted. In less than a minute the waiter returned with an entire unopened box of Sardi's matchbooks.

"This will make a nice souvenir," Phyllis said as she handed it to me. "This is going to be a collector's item."

"I'm going to tell Ingrid that if she ever so much as removes one of these books of matches, I'm going to break her arm," I said as I tucked the box safely inside my briefcase.

Mr. B approached the table just in time to hear my last few words and hesitated a moment, looking from me to Phyllis. I don't know if he thought I was threatening her or what, but the situation tickled Phyllis, and she threw back her head and laughed that famous laugh for probably the fiftieth time that day. But that one was from her heart.

Mr. B sat down and we ordered dinner, but it was not an enjoyable occasion. The conversation was all business. I was glad when it ended. Phyllis made it an early night, as we'd been on the road since early that morning.

The next day, Phyllis spent a good deal of time on the phone with Warde and Stephanie. We'd only been gone a couple of days, but she missed them and wanted to know how the play was going. When I came into the suite, Phyllis had some new publicity photos that she was scrutinizing.

"What do you think?" she asked as she handed me a "contact sheet" of small pictures, along with a magnifying glass. *Who travels with a magnifying glass?*

I looked at them carefully. Some were head shots and some full body. She had tamed the fright wig and in the head shots she actually looked pretty. Since her face-lift, she wanted pictures that were a little more glamorous. I didn't know which to choose.

"You always take a good picture," I said. "This is a whole new image."

Sure, she'd made her living poking fun at herself as a flat-chested, skinny-legged, funny-looking misfit, but what woman doesn't want to be pretty? I couldn't blame her for flaunting her new face. I shook my head as I handed her back the photo sheet and the magnifying glass. "I think you could use any one of them."

She looked at them one more time, then set the sheet aside and picked up the schedule.

"Have you called the Playboy Club-Hotel in New Jersey?" she asked.

"Yes, their limo will pick us up tomorrow at noon."

"Okay. I'm going to rest awhile and go over my act. Come back at seven. You told Jimmy seven-thirty, right?"

"Right."

This would be an easy show. There was no music, just her stand-up act for a convention of beauticians. "My favorite audience!" she'd quipped when Roy told her about it. It was, actually, perfect for her. She had a whole slew of jokes on the subject: "I went into a beauty parlor that had a money-back guarantee; they paid me in advance." "My going to a beauty parlor makes about as much sense as an ashtray on a motorcycle." "I'm on my fifth year of a five-day beauty plan." And about her hairdresser, Mr. Nancy: "Hell, he's prettier than I am! One day he was teasing my hair and it bit him!" That always got a huge laugh.

I had about four hours before Jimmy would pick us up, so I went for a walk. Being in New York alone wasn't as much fun as it had been with Karen, but I still liked looking in the big department stores. The weather was downright cold. I went into Saks Fifth Avenue and Lord and Taylor as much to get warm as to actually shop. I couldn't fit another thing in my suitcase anyway—besides, I'd spent all my money on Christmas.

When I got back to the hotel, I ordered a club sandwich from room service. It was still way above my price range, but I couldn't afford any of the restaurants, and I wasn't dressed for fine dining. The sandwich was a perfectly good, five-dollar sandwich, although it had cost nearly four times that. Plus tip. Plus service charge. I was glad we were leaving in the morning. I couldn't afford to eat in New York!

Jimmy was waiting for us when we got downstairs that evening. The hotel doorman hurried ahead of us and opened the limo door. Phyllis got in the back and I stood there for a few seconds waiting for her to scoot over. She didn't. When the doorman realized she wasn't going to scoot, he closed her door and opened the front passenger door for me. I handed him the small suitcase and the wig box to put in the trunk and was grateful for the warm blast of air coming from the car's heater. Even standing outside in that icy air for just a minute made me appreciate the warm car. Wow, what did people do who had to take the subway and walk to work?

The show was as simple as we'd expected. Phyllis did her act, was wildly applauded, got a standing ovation, and was done. She actually did something unusual—she wore her costume back to the hotel. There was no reason to change—she just put on her long fur coat. I grabbed the little suitcase with her street clothes and the wig box from the dressing room, and we were in the limo almost as soon as the applause had died down.

Phyllis opened the door to her suite and said goodnight, and I turned thankfully into my room. Although the hour was not late, I was ready for bed.

The next day, the Playboy limo arrived at noon and the chauffeur managed to fit most of our suitcases into the trunk. Again, the rest went into the back seat beside Phyllis, so I rode up front with the chauffeur. I enjoyed looking out the window as we passed from the city into the countryside. In less than an hour, we reached the Playboy Club-Hotel in New Jersey—a warm retreat in a frozen world. The sprawling hotel seemed to have been built right into the hillside. The wood-and-stone interior conveyed a wonderful coziness; huge picture windows looked out on ski slopes. For the next two days we would not have to do anything except a brief rehearsal and the shows.

During the time we were there, I barely went outside, content to sit in the lounge and watch the skiers gliding down the hills. That was partly due to the fact that I didn't have real cold-weather clothes or snow boots. Packing for the varied climates had been a challenge. Had we been going only to the East, I would have brought all winter clothes. As it was, I had to pack half for the warm weather in Puerto Rico, and half for the cold weather in New York, New Jersey, and Chicago. So for the cold weather I relied mostly on my Spanish cape, which was nearly as warm as any of Phyllis's furs, I was sure.

As a matter of fact, Phyllis had tried to give me one of her furs, a calf-length, mink paw coat. She never really liked it, and I think she bought it more for the novelty than anything. Her favorite coat was the soft, gray chinchilla. I loved that coat, too. Just holding it made me feel all warm inside. For fun, Phyllis wore the lynx and sometimes the strange-looking yak with the long, stringy hair, which I knew in my heart was really yarn, but I'd never seen her wear the mink paw.

"What are you going to wear in New York?" Phyllis had asked me when the trip started to jell. "You've never been there in the winter. Do you have a warm coat?"

"I have my Spanish cape," I told her. "That's good and warm."

"What about a fur? Nothing keeps you warm like fur."

"No, no fur." I had to smile. A fur coat in Southern California where I could wear it only a few times a year would be extravagant indeed.

"I have a coat you could have," Phyllis went on. "Come into the wardrobe."

Obediently, I put down the schedule we were revising and followed her into the wardrobe room, which I still found rather spooky.

Phyllis headed for the fur rack. "Here it is," she said, slipping a coat off the hanger. "Try this on."

"There's no way it's going to fit me," I protested. "I'm much bigger than you."

"It's too big for me," Phyllis insisted. "Try it."

I slipped into the coat and found that what was midcalf on Phyllis hit me right at the knees. The sleeves were a good inch short of my wrists, and although I could, technically, wear it, I couldn't move.

"Button it," Phyllis urged.

"I don't think I can."

"Sure you can," she persisted. I buttoned the middle button. I couldn't breathe.

"Perfect!" she exclaimed.

I shook my head.

"Come look in the mirror."

I stood in front of the full-length mirror and saw exactly what I thought I would see—a woman wearing a coat three sizes too small.

"It won't work," I said as I shrugged out of it.

"Are you sure? I never wear it. You could have it. You need a fur coat."

She was certainly no more disappointed than I. Wouldn't I love to have a fur coat!

"I wouldn't be able to move, and if I sneezed, the whole thing would rip at the seams." I slowly hung it on the rack. "No, but thank you. My cape will have to do. Besides," I said to change the subject, "I'm already taking two suitcases of clothes. I just wouldn't have room for a fur coat."

It had been a lovely gesture, and one I appreciated. When I told Ingrid about it later she stared at me in disbelief. "Why didn't you take it?" she cried.

"Ingrid, I couldn't wear it!"

"But I could have!"

Which was true. Ingrid stood a few inches taller than Phyllis but was quite slender. The mink paw coat would have fit her to a T.

27

From the Playboy Club-Hotel we went directly to San Juan, Puerto Rico, for a two-week engagement at the Caribe Hilton. I looked forward to the sun and warm lovely beaches. However, it didn't turn out to be as idyllic as I'd envisioned.

Things got off to a bad start when Phyllis decided to fly to San Juan a day ahead of schedule. Our original plan called for us to travel on Monday, arriving there at about six in the evening. But on Saturday night, between shows at the Playboy Club, she said, "Why don't we go down tomorrow? There's no point hanging around here where it's cold and snowy, when we could be enjoying the lovely warm weather in Puerto Rico."

I agreed. I never liked cold weather.

"Phone them in the morning and tell them we're coming," she instructed.

It sounded easy. I mentally went over all the things I'd have to do—change the plane reservations, alert the limousine, get in touch with the hotel in San Juan, call Mr. B, who had planned to spend Sunday afternoon with Phyllis, and let the bellman know to get the bags out of storage. (We had to haul all forty suitcases with us because there wasn't any central place to leave the ones we didn't need. I'd had the bellman put the extra thirty-four bags in the storeroom.)

By then traveling had become fairly routine. No longer did I toss and turn the night before a trip with nightmares of missed flights or unmade reservations. I'd become used to changing flights at the next-to-the-last minute due to Warde's nasty habit of waiting until the afternoon before we were to leave for a trip, then strolling into the office and saying something like "By the way, Madam has decided she wants to take a later flight tomorrow," and strolling out again. It was one of the ways he used to prove that he could manipulate Phyllis.

The fact that it also made life difficult for the help, as he referred to us, was icing on the cake. The first time he did this, it threw me for a loop. I hit the panic button trying to make five phone calls at the same time.

Gradually, however, I got things down to a science. The first call was to Jimmy Retty, Phyllis's travel agent, who always found us a flight, even at the very last minute. Then I called the promoter of the event, or wherever she was appearing, to let them know we'd be arriving at a different time than originally scheduled, then I notified the limousine service on each end, and let the hotel know the change in expected arrival time. Of course, that often caused problems and inconvenienced people all the way down the line—another bonus for Warde.

On the trip to Puerto Rico, however, I had no travel agent to smooth the way. My first priority was to see if we could actually get the same flight a day earlier; next I had to notify the Caribe Hilton that we'd be arriving Sunday evening and make sure they met us at the airport with the limousine and baggage wagon.

Changing the flight turned out to be no problem. The stumbling block came when I contacted the hotel in

Puerto Rico. I had realized after I returned from the Foreign Service how much we in this country take our telephones for granted. It's almost unheard of to call a number and not get through. However, I was quickly reminded of the vagaries of foreign telephone systems when I contacted the hotel operator and asked how to reach Puerto Rico.

"Oh, you'll have to go through the operator," she told me.

"Isn't this the operator?" I asked. Perhaps I'd dialed room service by mistake.

"No, I mean the big operator. I'll connect you."

The big operator placed the call and after two minutes of clicking and buzzing, she informed me that the circuits were busy and I should try again. I tried again. And again. After nearly two hours of persistent calling, I finally got the desired response—a ringing phone—at the other end.

"Caribe Hilton," a voice said in heavily accented English.

"Hello!" I answered brightly, relieved to have gotten through at last.

"Caribe Hilton," the voice repeated. My heart sank. I had the distinct impression that the person didn't understand the word "hello." I repeated it.

"Hello?" the voice queried.

The connection had been tenuous in the first place, then the sounds of eggs frying washed over the line.

"Hello!" I shouted, but I was talking to a dial tone.

The hotel operator was sympathetic and continued to put me through to the big operator at regular intervals. At last I was once again rewarded by the sound of a ringing telephone.

"Caribe Hilton."

I tried a different tack. "*Hable Inglés?*" I asked.

"Eh?"

"*Hable Inglés?*" I shouted.

Silence greeted me. I didn't know if she was trying to come up with the correct answer to the question, or if she had gone to find someone who *hable'd Inglés*. A moment later another voice came over the line.

"*Hable Inglés?*" I queried again.

"*Si.*"

"*Bueno,*" I said, thereby exhausting my entire command of the Spanish language. "This is Phyllis Diller's secretary."

"Eh?" the voice said.

"Phyllis Diller!"

"Oh."

I took a fresh approach. "Is the manager there?" I asked it slowly and loudly which, of course, is a time-tested method for making oneself clearly understood to people who don't speak English.

"Manager?"

"Manager!" I shouted. "I want to talk to the manager!" I said "manager" even more loudly and even more slowly, clearly enunciating each syllable.

"*Momento,*" the voice replied, and I heard the telephone being set down. Several minutes passed. We didn't have all day. In fact, we were leaving for the airport in less than an hour. Finally, a new voice came on the line.

"Do you speak English?" I asked.

"Yes."

"Thank heaven!"

"Eh?"

"Never mind! Listen, this is Phyllis Diller's secretary. We're going to be arriving tonight instead of tomorrow."

"Who?"

"Phyllis Diller!"

"Oh."

"You know, the lady who is going to entertain in your hotel. Phyllis Diller!"

"Yes?" came the doubtful affirmation. The fact that every response from the other end was a monosyllable had begun to disturb me.

"Is the manager there?" I asked again.

"At lunch."

"Oh. Well, do you understand? Phyllis Diller is going to be coming tonight instead of tomorrow. You have to have the limousine and baggage car at the airport tonight at six o'clock. Okay?"

"Phyllis Diller," he repeated doubtfully.

"Yes. Tonight at six. Please have the limousine meet us at the airport. Eastern Airlines."

"What?"

I knew I had just confused the issue beyond retrieval.

"Never mind. Just have the limousine at the airport at six tonight to meet Phyllis Diller. And tell the manager!"

"Okay."

"Promise?" I asked, but the line had already gone dead. I figured I'd been talking to a brick wall, but it was too late to do anything else. We had to forge ahead.

"Did you get through?" Phyllis asked when I went to her room.

"I think so. I talked to someone who said he spoke English, but I'm not sure he understood."

"Did you tell them it was for me?"

"I did."

"Well, that'll be okay then."

Her faith was a great deal stronger than mine, but I decided not to press the point. We'd see what happened when we landed in Puerto Rico.

What happened when we landed in Puerto Rico was that every English-speaking person on the plane transformed into a native-born Puerto Rican. We became the only English-speaking people in the entire airport. I made sure that Phyllis and I stayed close together, and there was no doubt she had the same idea. For one thing, I had both of our passports and all the money. For another, she had been drinking on the plane and was none too steady on her feet. The flight crew had done their best to keep her champagne glass full while Phyllis seemed determined to get it empty. The only thing in our favor so far was that no one had recognized Phyllis, so we didn't have to keep a lookout for eager fans descending on us.

We followed the flow of people and eventually ended up in a large, long, baggage area where people from apparently hundreds of previous flights were gathered. It was a mob.

"Where are the bags?" Phyllis asked.

"I'm not sure yet." I scanned the overhead signs for something that said Eastern Airlines but without any luck.

"Do you see anyone who was on our flight?" she whispered as if she didn't want people to overhear.

"They've gone," I said. I felt as if we had entered the Twilight Zone.

"Where's the limousine?" she asked.

From the baggage area I could see a lot of taxis and vehicles pulled up at the curb, but nothing that remotely resembled a limousine. From where I stood, many of them barely resembled automobiles.

"Not here."

"Did you call them?" she asked with the persistence of the inebriated.

"I called them. They'll be here. Right now I've got to find our bags."

During the entire conversation I'd been scanning the area for newly arrived bags. I was somewhat alarmed by the many large signs that proclaimed "Do Not Leave Luggage Unattended" in several languages. I decided to check out the baggage area farther afield since nothing seemed to be happening in our vicinity.

"I'm going down to the other end," I told Phyllis. "You wait right here by this pillar where I can find you."

"Don't leave me!"

"I have to find the luggage. I'll be right back."

She peered at me doubtfully. "You better get the bags. And the limousine."

Oh, yeah, there's a good idea. Perspiration started running down my back. It was humid in Puerto Rico, but that wasn't the reason.

I nodded curtly and started off, torn between finding the limousine, whose driver could help with the bags, and the fear of leaving the luggage, which was still nowhere in sight, unattended. I opted for the former and ran outside for a quick look. Heavens, it was hot! I looked over the parking area from one end to the other. No limousine in sight. I dashed back inside to find Phyllis right where I'd left her.

"No limo," I said.

"Why don't you get the bags," she asked, as if the thought had just occurred to her.

"Good idea. Wait here. I'll see if I can find which conveyor belt is ours."

"Don't leave me!" She reached out and grabbed my arm, which told me how nervous she was—Phyllis did not encourage physical contact.

"I have to get the bags."

Reluctantly she released me. "All right." She looked so small and helpless standing next to the pillar, like somebody's grandmother (which in fact she was) feeling helpless in a foreign country.

"I'll be right back," I said.

Several of the conveyor belts were loaded with bags. It remained for me to find the one with ours. I picked the one which had most recently shuddered to life and watched for something familiar, heaving a sigh of relief when I spotted one or our big, plaid suitcases emerging. I waded through the group of people and started tugging luggage off the belt. I soon had a mountain of bags and realized that I couldn't keep my eyes on both the bags coming out on the belt and the ones surrounding me. Phyllis would have to help.

Dragging over the first of the bags, I deposited them next to her. "You watch the luggage," I told her. Some perverse little voice inside of me said, *Yeah, it's time she started doing some work around here.*

I collected the bags as quickly as I could, worrying each time I turned my back that one would disappear.

"How many do we have now?" Phyllis asked each time I added another to the group.

"You count 'em," I told her with uncharacteristic curtness. I already knew, of course, but I figured it wouldn't hurt to have some corroboration.

"That's thirty-six," she said when I returned with the next pair. "How many do we have?"

"Forty."

"What's missing?"

"I'll check in a minute. There's more coming out." I'd spotted the two wig boxes and wanted to snatch them before they were out of reach. In another minute, I had the complete set.

"I'm going to phone the hotel," I said, although the idea was impractical. For one thing, I didn't have any of the local currency. For another, I didn't know how their phones worked. And, of course, I still didn't speak the language.

Surprisingly, Phyllis vetoed the idea. The champagne was wearing off, thank heaven. "Let's just get a cab."

"I don't think we can get all this in a cab." Boy, was I

wishing we'd spent that extra day at the Playboy Club-Hotel!

Just then an angel appeared in the guise of a perfectly ordinary porter. "Taxi?" he asked.

"Yes!" Phyllis and I answered in unison.

"Big taxi!" he said, his face splitting into a huge grin. "You wait," he instructed and he scuttled outside.

We waited.

In five minutes the porter returned with a man in tow. "He owns wagon," the porter said, and began to pile bags onto his handcart. The wagon owner looked more like he owned a pig farm, but if he could get us into town, I really didn't care.

"Where are you going?" he asked in better English than they apparently spoke at the hotel.

"Caribe Hilton. There was supposed to be a limousine here to meet us," I added in some forlorn hope that he would say, "Yes, there is a limousine here," but he only nodded and said "Caribe Hilton."

Phyllis tugged at my sleeve. "Watch the bags!" she said in an anxious, Pooh-like whisper. "Which ones?" Part of them were still sitting on the ground, while the others were being trundled off by the only English-speaking porter in San Juan.

"All of them."

By that time the owner of the wagon had tucked several bags under his massive arms and was making his way outside.

"You go with those," I told Phyllis. "I'll stay with these." She hesitated a moment. "Quick," I urged as the driver disappeared around a corner.

I knew she was loath to go by herself, but after only another moment's hesitation, she scurried after the man carrying away our luggage.

I picked up a couple of the smaller bags as I waited

for our porter to return. He and the driver came back at the same time, and between the three of us we managed to wheel, drag, and tote the remainder of our luggage.

As we neared the curb, I spotted Phyllis standing next to a fairly decent-looking Volkswagen minibus. The driver quickly piled the rest of the bags inside as the porter told me, "Now I get taxi for you."

"No. No taxi," Phyllis said. Then she whispered to me, "I'm not letting this van out of my sight!"

"We'll ride with the bags," I told the porter. He repeated this to the driver in Spanish and they both shrugged.

"Tip him," Phyllis instructed as she clambered up the high step and wedged herself into the back seat between the kitchen bag and a wig box. "A lot!" she added as I wrestled the petty-cash purse out of my handbag.

I extracted two twenty-dollar bills—about double the normal tip even in the U.S.—and handed them over.

The man grinned and said, "*Gracias, senorita! Muchas gracias!*" He added a "*Vaya con Dios!*" as he carefully closed the door. "*Gracias, gracias!*" he called again as we pulled away from the curb.

"I think I overdid it," I muttered.

"It was worth it."

As we drove through miles of cultivated fields toward the city, I tried not to consider the fact that the Caribe Hilton obviously didn't know we were arriving that evening. It was grim comfort to be proven right. When we arrived at the hotel, we were part of a small parade of cars and taxis. Our driver angled into a vacant spot that featured "No parking, stopping or standing" signs and proceeded to do all three.

As he began to unload the bags, I clambered out of the van and held the door for Phyllis.

"I'm not budging from here until you get the manager," she informed me. She crossed her arms and settled herself even deeper into the space between the suitcases. I wondered if she had taken those "Watch your luggage" signs too seriously and hoped she wasn't going to make a life-long habit of it.

"The manager," she repeated firmly as I hesitated. The driver unloaded the suitcases, and I pushed my way into the lobby. A mob of guests crowded the front desk. I elbowed my way to the front, determinedly ignoring the hostile glares and ominous mutterings. I leaned across and grabbed the nearest clerk by the arm.

"Get me the manager," I said in a calm but firm voice. "Now!"

He rewarded me with a blank stare. "The *manager*!" I repeated and raised my voice. "*Ahora*! Now!"

The clerk followed the blank stare with a look of consternation, but as I let go of his sleeve, he stepped backward through a door marked "Employees Only." Except that it said it in Spanish. I would give him thirty seconds, then I would follow him through that door. I was saved this painful necessity by his surprisingly speedy return with someone I was only too happy to assume was the manager.

"Listen," I started, "Phyllis Diller is here. She's in a van outside because you didn't send the limousine to the airport like you were supposed to. She wants to be shown to her room right now."

"Phyllis Diller?" his eyebrows shot up toward his hairline.

"Yes."

"Why wasn't I told?" he asked in an injured tone. He glanced at a book and held a brief conference with one of the other captives behind the desk.

"I will come," he said as he slipped around the end of the counter and trotted behind me out to the van.

"Ah, Miss Diller! You are here!" he effused.

Now that things were about to be rectified, she smiled sweetly.

"But, alas, your room is not ready." He did a wonderful imitation of an unctuous hotel manager, wringing his hands in distress and making little clucking noises. Perhaps it wasn't an imitation. Perhaps he was the genuine article.

"I will put you in a room where you can wait!" The idea seemed to have come to him so unexpectedly that his whole face brightened. "Yes! You can wait until your room is ready. Yes?"

"That will be fine," Phyllis told him.

"And those bags," he continued as he waved to our traveling luggage shop. "We will put those in our baggage room."

"No," Phyllis said. "The bags will come with us."

"All of them?"

"Yes. They are my costumes. I need them."

"Oh." He eyed the mountain of luggage as though it might have plans to take over the hotel, but he did not argue further. He waved toward the main door and several bellmen emerged. He spoke rapidly in Spanish, explaining, no doubt, that these two crazy women needed all this luggage to go with them to their room because they had a lot of clothes. As they began to load the bags onto their carts, I took a moment to deal with the van driver.

"How much?" I asked. He named an amount that I figured was quadruple what it should have been, but I wasn't in any position to quibble. I forked over the cash and added a sizeable tip, and found myself once again being blessed as he pocketed the small fortune and leaped into his trusty Volkswagen van. "*Adios y gracias*!" he called merrily as he pulled into the tangle of traffic and shot across three lanes of traffic, ignoring the blaring horns.

I turned back in time to see our luggage caravan disappearing into the cool interior of the hotel. I followed.

Eventually we were shown to our rooms. They were connecting, much to my dismay, but at least they were large and airy, with lots of closet space.

I stared glumly at our stack of luggage. "I guess we'd better do something with all these suitcases." I would have to sort them—costumes to be transported backstage, clothes to be unpacked for our two-week stay, and suitcases with the cold-weather clothes to be put at the back of the closet. Although it was not an arduous task, it was one of those petty things that wears on a person. I was not in the mood.

"But first," Phyllis said, "call room service and order two piña coladas. Have you ever had one?"

"No. What's a piña colada?"

"I first had them when I was down here filming a movie with Bob Hope. You can't come to Puerto Rico and not have a piña colada."

By the time we finished unpacking and stashing the suitcases, we'd each polished off three piña coladas, which turned out to be a wonderful frothy mixture of pineapple and coconut and rum.

Mostly rum.

Puerto Rico and I were going to get along just fine.

28

While we were in Puerto Rico, I reached the conclusion that Warde was not totally useless—he did have a place in the scheme of things and it was, surprisingly, slightly higher on the evolutionary ladder than pond scum. I realized that because Phyllis never went anywhere alone, I would have to go with her every time she wanted to go anyplace, no matter what time of the day or night. From the time Phyllis got up until the time we went to bed, unless she was in the bathroom or onstage, we were inseparable.

Phyllis had been there twice before, filming movies with Bob Hope, so there were places and people she wanted to revisit. We had drinks at El Convento—the old convent that had been transformed into a lovely hotel. We ate lunch at her favorite hole-in-the-wall restaurant and spent one entire afternoon shopping and going crazy over the handcrafts we found.

"Look at these embroidered shirts!" Phyllis crowed as she held up a man's white shirt, decorated with elaborate stitching. "I'm going to get them for the boys." So saying, she picked out six shirts, two for each of Warde's sons and two for Perry.

I was loving all the beads and embroidery. I ended up getting a large necklace of wooden beads and macramé. It had a cross on it. It wasn't until years later that I found out it was a rosary. *Oops!* I also got a large cloth bag that would serve very well as a beach bag. It looked like a horse blanket. It was sturdy and would hold a lot of stuff.

Another afternoon we went into a jewelry store where Phyllis, in less than an hour, spent what I considered to be an ungodly sum on things she didn't need and several she later decided she didn't even like.

The store owner either recognized Phyllis or realized she was a serious customer because nearly as soon as she began browsing, he went over and put the "Closed" sign on the door. He pulled out a tray of beautiful necklaces, but Phyllis told him that she didn't wear necklaces.

"Let me look at those rings," she said.

He pulled out an assortment of rings ranging from fairly plain to large and flashy.

"I'd like to try that one," she said, pointing to a large gold ring that was sort of a modified S-shaped dome. "Yes, I like this." She later referred to it as her "golden turd."

"Let me see your lapis lazuli," she said next. I'd previously heard it pronounced laz-*uli,* but the jeweler confirmed her pronunciation of *laz*-uli was correct. She chose another ring and a bracelet, too. Next she pored over the entire case of rings, earrings, and bracelets, but nothing there struck her fancy.

After that he showed her some unset stones, including a light-blue topaz.

"I thought topaz was yellow," I told the jeweler. I had a lovely, smoky-topaz ring I'd bought in South Africa.

"It comes in several shades," he said.

I was glad I didn't care much about jewelry. I would never understand it and couldn't afford it anyway. Phyllis ended up buying several pieces, including the blue topaz.

When all her purchases were bagged and the total rung up, Phyllis said, "Write the man a check."

I'd been watching this spending spree with a mixture of awe and disbelief. *Surely she's not going to get all of this.* At home she had begun to scrimp and save pennies in the most ludicrous ways. Phyllis told Val to buy only the brand of toothpaste that was on sale and the same went for hand lotion, shampoo, and other sundries. Also, we were told that "the house" would no longer supply cookies at breaks. If we wanted a snack, we were to bring our own. By practicing these small economies, she saved a couple of dollars a week, and now she turned around and spent an enormous amount on a whim. Granted, it was her money to do with as she liked, but this was ridiculous.

I snatched the checkbook from the petty-cash purse and with clenched teeth wrote the check for somewhere north of $6,000. Signing "Phyllis Diller" with a flourish, I tore it out of the checkbook and with a tight smile, handed it over to the store owner.

I wanted to say something, but it would have been a long swim back to California.

My dream of spending days lolling on the beach had been quashed, not only by the drastic curtailment of my free time, but also by the fact that the balmy tropical breezes, which made the palm trees sway so prettily, also blew sand everywhere. Between the wind and the humidity, those lovely looking Caribbean beaches were decidedly unpleasant. Besides that, there were the rats. Yes, big rats. They hung out at night by the pool—I'd pointed them out to Phyllis as we made our way backstage, and after that we did a pretty good imitation of a race-walk across the pool area on our way to the showroom.

"I've never seen rats like that," I said.

"Oh, I have. Some of them even had four legs!"

The wind killed my interest in lying on the beach. And lounging by the pool, knowing there were rats lurking in the landscaping? No, thank you! So, I used the hour or two in the morning to work before Phyllis got up.

During the afternoon, or whenever we had an idle moment, I coached Phyllis on her lines for the play she would be doing at Pheasant Run Theater the next month. After *Forty Carats* closed with Warde and Stephanie, Phyllis would star in a play—*Composition in Black and Blue*—that had been written expressly for her by one of her comedy writers, Jules Tasca. It was his first play, and Phyllis had been looking for ways to branch out into other fields of show business. The play seemed to be the perfect opportunity for them both. We didn't run lines as often as we should have, but Pheasant Run was still almost a month away, and there were two weeks in Hot Springs, Arkansas, yet to come. Why worry?

Phyllis felt perfectly free to make changes in the script just as she sometimes rewrote the jokes she bought. The play was a horse of a somewhat different color, I thought, but it didn't stop Phyllis from crossing out a line or changing the wording to something she considered funnier.

We'd been in San Juan nearly a week when Mr. B called from nearby St. Thomas in the Virgin Islands, where he had a winter house.

"Why don't you come over for a visit?" he asked Phyllis.

The idea appealed to her, and he assured us that flights took only a few minutes and left regularly. Phyllis agreed that on Monday, her day off, we'd fly over for the day. I was relieved that Phyllis declined his offer to stay overnight, not only because it would have involved packing, but I never was comfortable staying in other people's houses, especially people I didn't know well.

On Monday morning, we took a taxi to the harbor,

where the pilot of a little seaplane prepared for departure. The aircraft was small, holding only ten or twelve, with one seat on each side of the aisle. We took our places in the front and a young couple sat behind us. They held hands across the aisle.

Phyllis looked at them. "Are you newlyweds?"

"No," he answered. "We've been married six months."

Phyllis laughed. "You're newlyweds."

The plane took off and was too noisy for further conversation. After we disembarked in St. Thomas, Phyllis turned around and said, "I hope you have a long and happy life together."

I don't know if they recognized her, but they smiled at her and each other. I hope her wish for them came true.

Mr. B, dressed in shorts and sandals, met us at dockside. His wife was with him and chattered brightly on the drive out to their house. She went a long way toward making him seem human. The house was small and sparsely furnished with rattan furniture. A typical beach house.

I changed into the bathing suit I'd stuffed into my recently purchased horse-blanket beach bag and headed down the stairs to the sand. I concluded we were on the leeward side of the island since the breeze was distinctly less than at the Caribe Hilton, and the water was the brilliant blue that I'd always seen on postcards. I pulled a large beach towel from my bag and stretched out on the smooth, white sand. With a sigh of relief, I closed my eyes and let the warm Caribbean sun do its magic. I felt my muscles relaxing as my brain slid into neutral. *Heaven!*

I must have dozed because the next thing I knew I heard voices. Mr. B's wife and a neighbor were trotting down the stairs, each holding a wicker basket.

"We thought you might be hungry," Mrs. B said and opened her basket to bring out a tray of sandwiches and a jug of iced tea. The neighbor spread a bright tablecloth on the sand and produced a plate of tropical fruit. We ate and chatted, but I was no longer relaxed. Anything I said would be repeated, so I had to parry as diplomatically as possible the neighbor's natural but probing questions about life with Phyllis Diller. I tried to talk about the Virgin Islands, but inevitably the conversation came back to Phyllis.

Suddenly Mrs. B said, "It's time to go in!" and they both jumped up and started gathering the remains of the picnic lunch.

"What's wrong?" I asked.

"No-see-ums," Mrs. B answered cryptically.

I looked from one to the other.

"They're little biting midges that come late in the afternoon," the neighbor explained. "You can barely see 'em, but they'll bite the hell out of you."

We trudged up the stairs and when we reached the house, Phyllis told me we'd be leaving for dinner shortly.

I changed back into the summer dress and sandals I'd worn on the plane and joined them in the living room for drinks. "Seven-Up, if you have it," I told Mrs. B when she asked what I'd like. Phyllis was drinking a martini. A little while later, Mr. B suggested we head to the restaurant.

Four others joined us on a lovely terrace overlooking the harbor. I never enjoyed socializing with Phyllis or her friends, and with her attorney along, I felt like I was on trial. It was not a time to kick back. A waiter opened wine and poured all around. When he reached me, I declined.

"Don't you drink?" one of the men asked me.

"Sometimes."

"Excellent wine," he commented as he nodded toward the bottle.

"No, thank you," I answered in what probably sounded like a very prim voice. I was keeping an eye on the time, because we were catching the last flight back to San Juan. The way the drinks were being thrown back, I had a hunch I might be the only person there who cared whether we made that flight or not.

Dinner was delicious, as I'd expected. Nobody noticed or cared that I didn't take part in the conversation. Phyllis was there and obviously the center of attention.

We had after-dinner coffee and more drinks. Once again I politely refused.

"Come on, have a drink," one of the guests urged.

I smiled and bit back the snarl that simmered just below the surface. This whole afternoon and evening, being with strangers who acted like friends, was wearing on me.

"You didn't even have a glass of wine with dinner," she pointed out. "One little drink won't hurt."

I was still casting about for a suitable but polite rejoinder when Mrs. B mercifully came to my rescue. "You don't understand," she said sweetly. "Robin is working."

I could have hugged her. At least there was one person who didn't think that just because I was wearing a sundress and eating a gourmet dinner in the Caribbean meant I was on vacation. I hadn't realized until then how tired I got from never, ever being able to relax. I always had to be on guard, be alert, have the next day's schedule in mind, be pleasant, be polite but firm, and become invisible when I was no longer necessary. I very seldom had time to myself. Phyllis called it "star sitting," and that summed it up nicely.

That night in bed I started analyzing my job and my life and my future. One thing for certain, I wasn't being paid nearly enough.

The second week in Puerto Rico Phyllis wanted to do something every day or every night. Several nights after her second performance, we went to a small club to catch the 2:00 A.M. show. Phyllis knew people from the old Bob Hope days when she'd done those films with him. After the show, they talked and drank. During the show, too, for that matter.

Of course, I had no part in this. Her friends were polite, but really all I could do was sit off to the side and keep paying for the drinks. We usually didn't get home before dawn. Thank goodness our next engagement was in Hot Springs, Arkansas, where there would be no nightclubs, and the only thing Phyllis would have to do would be to work on that script for the play at Pheasant Run.

29

Phyllis finished her two weeks in Puerto Rico on Sunday night and we left at noon on Monday for The Vapors Club in Hot Springs, Arkansas. The Caribe Hilton limo drove us to the airport in style, even though the limo was stuffed from stem to stern with suitcases. A far cry from our arrival in a VW minivan driven by a man I still thought of as a pig farmer. At the airport in Hot Springs, the rental car awaited, just as Roy had arranged. Our flight got in at 6:30 p.m. after two plane changes.

The Taylor-Rosamund Motel, where we would be staying, was just across the street from The Vapors Club, so a limo wasn't practical. I would be the chauffer for the next two weeks. I didn't mind because I anticipated—correctly as it turned out—that Phyllis would be amenable to my going off by myself once in a while.

The Vapors would not be a demanding engagement. Being the only show in town, literally, it sold out every night, with no promotions or public appearances necessary. Phyllis had two shows each night, with an hour in between.

Some nights we'd have dinner delivered to the dressing room. Other nights Phyllis cooked dinner before we went over. She was a "hit-or-miss" cook. She never used a recipe and made things up as she went along. Sometimes the results were quite good; other times I could hardly choke them down. She loved making "garbage soup," a compilation of leftovers. She claimed to put everything in except lettuce and Jell-O. The leftovers came from our dressing room dinners, but even on past occasions when I'd had dinner with her in a restaurant, she was never shy about getting a doggie bag.

"After all," she pointed out, "they're just going to throw it away."

So I never knew what I'd be eating on any given night. *All part of the adventure*, I told myself.

Each night we drove the two-tenths of a mile from the top of the parking lot across the street to the stage door at the back of the club.

"I have an idea," Phyllis said one night. "How about if we drive over there and then back up coming home and see if the odometer goes back down." We laughed about the idea of turning the car in after ten days with less than ten miles on it. It didn't work.

"Oh, well," Phyllis said. "It was a fun idea."

Or maybe not, I thought, because backing the car back up the steep driveway at the motel in the dark seemed like an invitation for disaster.

Hot Springs sits on the edge of a national forest, and one day I asked Phyllis if I could take the car and get out for a couple of hours. "I just want to go for a drive through the forest," I told her. "Would you like to get out, too?"

Surprisingly, she liked the idea. Surprising because Phyllis did not like to be idle. If she wasn't with friends or family, or getting ready for a trip or performance, she used her free time working on her act, talking to her manager or agent, or doing something productive. Just driving around in a car was not her idea of a good time. Nevertheless, we drove through the hills and the trees and enjoyed chatting. We talked about Puerto Rico.

"I couldn't believe the wind in San Juan. That one day I went to the beach, the sand stuck to my suntan lotion and the wind blew my hair into my eyes," I told her.

"You might consider a wig," she said.

"I have a wig. It's long, dark hair. What would happen if we got it mixed up and you went onstage in a long, dark wig?"

"They'd think I was Cher!" She had a snappy comeback for everything. Phyllis always could see the humor.

As we drove back through the town, I told her I wanted to stop at the drugstore.

"I'll come in with you," she said.

I was apprehensive, but nobody bothered us. We walked through the store like everyone else. I even found some perfume I'd used years ago that I thought was out of production. It probably was an old bottle, but I bought it anyway. Phyllis picked up a few little things for the girls—some nail polish for Susie, bubble bath for Stephanie, and a little stuffed panda to send to Sally. Just like any parent who goes on a trip, she liked to bring presents home for her children.

I enjoyed the respite from the hectic lifestyle in San Juan. Phyllis had planned to put those two weeks in Hot Springs to good use, memorizing her lines for the coming play. However, rather than study the script, she spent a great deal of time on the phone with Warde and Stephanie. The days slipped by quickly, and as nearly as I could tell, Phyllis was no better prepared than she had been four weeks earlier.

Two days before we left, I spent an entire afternoon repacking our luggage. Phyllis told me that Stephanie had agreed to take some of it with her back to L.A. I didn't know if Steph would take as many as twenty suitcases—I doubted it—but at least she could take the wig boxes and costume bags. I hoped she'd take Phyllis's summer clothes, too.

On our last day in Hot Springs, Phyllis and I sorted everything, tying little ribbons on the suitcases that I wanted Stephanie to take. For the play, Phyllis would be wearing her own street clothes, so as far as I was concerned, we could've gotten rid of most of the luggage. I figured Stephanie would balk at more than half-a-dozen, but I would try. (Actually, she was a good sport, taking ten bags, so we were down to thirty, but then had to add in Warde's, so back up to thirty-four. Still, that was an improvement.)

In the morning, I settled the bill for our two rooms, piled everything into the car, and we headed to the airport. We were finally on the last lap of that marathon jaunt. Our flight made a connection through Memphis, and I fervently hoped that when we landed in Chicago there would be a limo waiting. Not only was the limo waiting, but Warde was there, too, and literally swooped Phyllis off her feet in a rather touching reunion.

The first night back at Pheasant Run, I accompanied Phyllis to the theater to watch Warde and Stephanie in *Forty Carats*. It was Stephanie's first play, and she wasn't sure if she wanted to make the stage a career. She had the looks—glorious red hair and a winning smile. Roy described her as a young Lauren Bacall. It would be silly of her to pass up such a golden opportunity, I thought, if she was at all interested. I'd grown up in Hollywood, and no matter how much the children of celebrities protest, the fact that their mommy or daddy is on a first-name basis with the producer, casting director, and agent opens doors. I'd seen firsthand the difficulty of even getting an introduction, let alone an audition, for someone who wasn't connected. For Stephanie, it was a heaven-sent chance.

After the show that night, the owner of the theater had a "closing-night party" at his house. For the first time in weeks I really enjoyed myself, knowing that when I wanted to leave, the car would take me back to the Inn, and I didn't have to worry about seeing Phyllis home.

The next morning, I awoke to falling snow, and I stayed snugly tucked up in my cozy bed in the loft, watching the large, silent flakes float down outside the tall windows. I luxuriated in the fact that I didn't have to anticipate what Phyllis would want to do that day. In fact, I figured that I wouldn't be hearing from Phyllis very much for the next week, and I was right. That first morning I used the in-room coffee pot and settled down with a book, perfectly content to let the day slip away. Phyllis would start rehearsal the next afternoon, and I wanted to enjoy my solitude while I had the chance.

I pottered around my little nest, munching on crackers and cheese I'd bought at the little "country store." The place reminded me of the Playboy Club-Hotel in Lake Geneva except that there were no luxurious grounds to prowl. We were right on the main highway. I had nothing to do at rehearsal, and after the first day I didn't bother to show up at the theater. However much I had looked forward to not having demands made on me every moment, I soon found the hours began to drag. I had nowhere to go outside of the little complex. We were miles from anywhere. Even going for a walk was out of the question, because there were no sidewalks beside the highway. Really, nowhere to walk at all. In addition to that, the snow fell almost daily. Pretty to look at from inside a warm room, but not at all nice to be trudging through.

Thank goodness for Jules Tasca. The playwright turned up the day before dress rehearsal for *Composition in Black and Blue*. Phyllis had invited him for opening night. At last I would have someone to talk to and eat with for a couple of days. (I had finally overcome my aversion to eating alone in restaurants. I still didn't enjoy it, but one can live on crackers and cheese for only so long.) I accompanied Jules to the dress rehearsal—the first rehearsal I'd seen since the initial one. Wow! The show was no further along than it had been a week earlier. Phyllis could not resist improvising, which threw the rest of the cast into confusion and uncertainty. The production became a hodgepodge, and even the director, a mild-mannered man, was losing patience.

That surprised me, because as long as I'd worked for Phyllis, she had exhibited the utmost professionalism. She was always prompt and always knew her lines, and she always did exactly as the director said.

After the dress rehearsal, Jules and I stopped in the coffee shop for dinner. He confided that he was disappointed in the way his play had turned out.

"Why don't you tell her?" I said. Even though I'd only met him the day before, I could tell he was not a forceful man. He wrote funny dialogue, but in person he was shy.

"What good would it do now?" he asked. "It's too late to do anything except go with it."

"Your first play, too," I lamented. I supposed that Phyllis thought she was improving the play by adding her personal touch, but it was a far cry from the original script Jules had sent her. She had even changed the title to *Subject to Change*. She thought that was appropriate because she had made so many changes.

"I'm glad my wife couldn't come after all," he said. "I don't think she would have enjoyed this."

"Are you going to call her?"

"No, I think I'll wait. Maybe it'll come together by tomorrow night."

Are we being just a tad optimistic?

Opening night went less badly than I anticipated, but there were obvious rough spots. Jules and I shared a booth with Warde and Stephanie, and I relaxed only when the ordeal ended. Afterward, there was a little party onstage for the cast and crew, but no one really felt much like celebrating.

"I think we'd better have a rehearsal in the morning," the director announced. No one disagreed.

Jules went to the rehearsal, but I saw no need for me to be there. I sat by the indoor swimming pool, reading and contemplating another three weeks of sitting around watching snow fall. It was late afternoon by the time I saw Jules.

"How'd it go?" I asked.

"Think I'll go swimming," he replied. As I watched Jules swim laps, I came to realize I'd fallen into the grip of the worst kind of ennui. The thought he'd be going back to his family the next day and I would be alone again made the next three weeks loom like an abyss.

It wasn't that I would miss Jules particularly. I was simply starved for company. I missed my friends. I thought with fondness about Bruce, the man I had met over the holidays at a party. As a photographer with his own studio, he enjoyed going to the beach and taking pictures of driftwood and seagulls. I enjoyed the beach, too--especially in California, where it wasn't windy and they didn't have rats. I would have liked it even better in summer, and the more I thought about sunshine and friends, the more melancholy I became.

There had been little to keep me busy during rehearsals except occasionally to take some fan mail to Phyllis in the theater. Once the show got under way, there would be absolutely nothing for me to do, because she would be coming into the theater only in the evening for the performance. In Puerto Rico and Hot Springs, I hadn't had more than a few minutes to myself on any given day. At Pheasant Run, I had entire days when the only person who spoke to me was the maid who cleaned the room and the waitress at the Kountry Kitchen, where I ate alone each night. The little shops were closed except for a couple of hours in the evening prior to show time. I seemed to be the only inhabitant of the whole place. I didn't even need to field phone calls because they went directly to Phyllis's house. By the time the play was in the middle of the first week, I decided to try to speak to Phyllis alone. This was going to be difficult since Warde came to the theater every night. He never left her side except when she was onstage. Unwittingly, Phyllis provided the way.

The director called a brief rehearsal for early afternoon several days after the play opened. Having nothing else to do, I went down to the theater.

As they wrapped up, Phyllis motioned to me. "I want you to come out to the house this afternoon. There are some things I need taken care of."

On the ride out to the house, she seemed withdrawn, gazing out the window at the snow-covered woods. I decided to wait until we had finished whatever work she had in mind to bring up the possibility of my going back to L.A. early.

As soon as we got into the house, Warde began bombarding Phyllis with messages. I went into the dining room, whose table was covered with what I'd long ago accepted as Phyllis's organized disarray, and began going through some of the papers. After a few minutes, Phyllis came in. She dictated some letters and handed me another stack to answer on my own, as I often did. She also had some phone calls she wanted me to make the next day, and I duly made notes of them.

"Ada," Warde said as he poked his head in the door. "Honey, do you want me to go get Chinese for dinner, or are you going to cook?"

Warde seemed to be on exceptionally good behavior. Perhaps he'd actually missed her while she was gone.

"I'll make something, Warde," Phyllis responded with less than her usual enthusiasm. The house was beautiful, but isolated. I wondered if she was beginning to get cabin fever, too, especially since Stephanie had left and it was just the two of them.

It became clear that I would stay for dinner. It should have been a pleasant break, but I cringed at the idea of eating dinner in that strained atmosphere. However, I told myself it wouldn't be a long meal because there wasn't much time before we had to leave for the theater. So I sat at the kitchen table and watched Phyllis cook. I knew it would be a bad time to bring up my request, but it might be the only chance I'd get to talk to Phyllis privately. There didn't seem to be an easy way to start, so I waited until she had the vegetables cooking and plunged in.

"Phyllis, you know we've been on the road since the middle of February," I started, waiting for a reaction.

"Warde, are we out of butter?" she called into the living room.

I heard a muffled reply and fiddled with the salt shaker, trying not to feel like an intruder.

"February twentieth," Phyllis said as she stirred leftovers on the stove.

"Yes, the twentieth," I said. "This play is going to last three more weeks, and there really isn't anything for me to do."

I hoped Phyllis would make it easy for me, but all she said was "the dishes are in that cupboard to your left." I began setting the table. Phyllis continued to stir and acted as though she hadn't heard me.

"You know, it's pointless for me to stay here," I went on. "All the work is piling up in L.A. You don't need me; Warde's with you; there aren't any interviews; I'm just sitting around waiting in case you want to dictate a couple of letters."

Warde chose that moment to put in an appearance. The timing could not have been worse.

"Warde, put butter on the shopping list, would you?" Phyllis said, then began serving dinner as Warde scrawled "butter" on a piece of paper on the counter.

She set the food on the table. Peas. I hated peas. They made me gag. Surely, I'd hit bottom.

We ate quickly and in silence, then it was almost time to leave. I tried to be helpful by washing the dishes while Phyllis put on her stage makeup and Warde hunted for the car keys.

Just as I put the last of the dishes in the drainer, Warde called out, "I'll start the car, honey." Phyllis came down the stairs almost simultaneously with the closing of the front door. Once again she was swathed in her white mink coat. I was still wearing the jacket I'd had on that afternoon when I'd gone down to rehearsal.

If I'd known I'd be out late, I would have brought my cape.

I'd turned out some of the lights as directed, leaving the living room and entrance hall lit, and was gearing up for the dash across the few feet of snow to the car when Phyllis spoke up.

"All right," she said as I reached for the door. "Call the airline tomorrow and make your reservations."

She sounded annoyed and defeated. I knew she was unhappy, but I was going berserk sitting in my room day after day with no one to talk to, eating all my meals alone, wearing the same clothes over and over, doing my laundry in the washbasin.

I didn't even wait until Phyllis went onstage. As soon as we got back to Pheasant Run, I bolted for my room. I called the airline and reserved a seat on the first nonstop flight to L.A. I arranged to have the theater car pick me up in the morning, and I called my parents to let them know I was coming home. It didn't take long to get everything packed, and I was back at the theater by the time the show ended to let Phyllis know what time I would be leaving. I couldn't believe how excited I was to be going home.

The next morning I got up early. I made the phone calls as Phyllis had instructed the night before, and got the correspondence in order. I left everything at the desk at the Inn, and the staff promised to take it to the theater later on. The car picked me up at the appointed time, and I arrived at the airport an hour early. Better to wait there than in my room at the Inn. The little room, which had seemed so cozy two weeks earlier, seemed like a prison cell—I knew every nook and cranny, every vagary of the heating system, every shade of pattern on the bedspread, the exact time the maid came to clean the room, where the carpet was patched, and exactly how far back I could tip the reclining chair without hitting the wall.

The airport seemed like a dear and welcoming world. There were people—lots of them—and noise and life. I checked my bags and, even though I still had to carry my typewriter and briefcase, I felt marvelously unencumbered. The gate agent recognized me from previous trips with Phyllis and upgraded my ticket to first class. I'd never flown first class by myself. And I wouldn't have to be "*en garde.*" I could get rip-roaring drunk and flirt with the good-looking man across the aisle, or put my mind in neutral and stare out the window for 1,500 miles, or simply curl up and take a nap. Getting drunk held no appeal, and there was no good-looking man across the aisle, so I turned the earphones on to the classical station and listened to Mozart while I watched the incredibly beautiful country slide slowly beneath our wings. I felt the tension of all those weeks slipping behind me, too.

30

A friend of Ingrid's had a party Saturday night. I plunged into the room full of people and reveled at being on my own again. I didn't have to keep track of Phyllis or consider where we had to be next or who was coming for an interview, or what time we'd have to get up in the morning, or any of the myriad details of "star sitting."

I gave myself a couple of days off and spent them with my parents, filling them in on the entire trip and basking in my own home, my own yard, my own family, and eating my mother's truly delicious cooking. *Why had I not appreciated that all these years?* With a few days of normal living, I was refreshed and ready to tackle the world.

When I went back to work, it felt as if I'd been gone forever. Maria, as always, was an eager audience, and at break time I regaled the staff with tales of our Puerto Rican adventures and Phyllis's play at Pheasant Run. I tackled the routine work with alacrity. The ordinariness of a routine had become enormously appealing.

I'd been back three days when Maria came to me, her eyes wide with apprehension. "Phyllis's attorney wants to talk to you."

Mr. B. The fact that he handled all the dirty work for Phyllis gave Maria the impression that whenever he called for any one of us personally, it had to be bad news. I stopped my search for the script Phyllis had asked me to find when she'd called the day before. I was in the billiards room at the time, one of the few rooms in the house without a phone.

"Tell him to hold on," I said and trotted back up the stairs and down the long hallway to the office. Mr. B's secretary was on the line.

"Hold, please," she whined in her nasal, New York accent that set my teeth on edge. I waited for about three minutes—approximately the same amount of time it had taken me to get back to the office. Tit for tat, I thought.

"Robin . . ." Mr. B's voice sounded hollow on the long-distance connection. "Phyllis asked me to call you about the raise we discussed." (I'd managed to bring up the matter when we were in St. Thomas.) "Miss Diller agrees that you deserve a raise. It'll be reflected in your next paycheck."

"How much are we talking about?" I asked.

He named a sum that certainly was not munificent, but at least it was a step in the right direction. I decided not to argue but to bring up the matter in another three months.

"There's something else," he continued. "You know, Phyllis is really unhappy that you deserted her in Chicago. She thinks you should have stuck with the job and stayed until she was ready to come home."

Deserted her? I was stunned. "I'm sorry to hear that," I said in a strangled voice. *Deserted her?* I hadn't deserted her—if anything, she had deserted me, leaving me stranded at the Inn day after day. What the hell was the woman thinking? She had hired me to work for her; she hadn't bought herself a slave.

"I'm sure it won't happen again," Mr. B said in the patronizing tone of a grade-school principal reprimanding an errant child.

I don't even remember saying good-bye. I just hung up. I sat for a few minutes looking out the window, gathering my thoughts.

Maria walked into the office after having stopped downstairs for a chat with Mary. "Are you all right?" she asked. "You're white as a sheet."

"I'm not sure." I told her what Mr. B had said.

Maria, as always, waxed philosophical. "By the time they get back from Chicago, Phyllis will have forgotten all about it."

I knew that wasn't true. Phyllis never forgot anything.

"Is Ingrid here?" I asked.

"No, she had an audition this afternoon. She's not coming in."

Ingrid was an aspiring actress and often went to casting calls. I was anxious to talk to her—she'd worked for Phyllis long enough to know all the previous secretaries. I hoped she might be able to give me some insight. When I got back to the apartment, Ingrid was home. I told her about the phone call. I paced back and forth as I spilled out the whole story.

"It's not as though I could have done anything for her," I said for probably the tenth time. "I mean, she has Warde with her, she does the play every night, and she's staying in a nice house. It's not as though we got together and worked every day. I just sat in my room day after day with nothing to do. It couldn't have made any difference to Phyllis whether I was there or not. And as for the work, it's all here in L.A."

Ingrid shrugged. "You know how she is."

"Yeah, that's the trouble. I probably haven't heard the end of this." We were silent for a few minutes while Ingrid fidgeted and I fumed.

"I just don't know what she expects," I said. "I did everything I could. I mean, I hadn't had a day off for weeks. I was going crazy!"

Ingrid started to say something, then stopped, then opened her mouth again and closed it.

"What?" I demanded.

"I shouldn't tell you this." She looked away and fiddled with her honey-blond hair.

"What?" I coaxed more gently.

"Well, you remember Corrine?"

"Corrine? Of course I remember Corrine!" I had never met Corrine, but I had heard about her from almost the first day I went to work for Phyllis. Corrine the Efficient. Corrine the Clever. Corrine the Perfect. She had been Phyllis's first secretary and had been with her about five years before moving on to Walt Disney Studios, where she held some kind of lofty position in keeping with her Incredible Brilliance and Unending Resourcefulness. I had never laid eyes on the woman, but I had seen pictures, and not only did she possess all the attributes of a saint (or so I understood from Phyllis and Val and even Ingrid, who still kept in touch with her), but she was beautiful. Ingrid, my own roomie, thought Corrine was the perfect secretary who could do no wrong under any circumstance. I hated the very idea of Corrine.

"What about Corrine?" I demanded in a voice that I struggled to keep calm. Even the mention of that woman's name drove my blood pressure up.

"I wasn't supposed to tell you."

"You weren't supposed to tell me what?" I asked in a deadly calm voice.

Ingrid squirmed. "The only reason I know is because Val had to call me for Corrine's number. She swore me to secrecy."Ingrid was making a list-ditch effort to avoid spilling the beans.

"Tell me."

She took a deep breath and plunged in. "Phyllis called Corrine and asked her to come back to work for her."

"She *what?*" I knew my voice carried out into the courtyard and probably to several surrounding apartments.

"It was after you left Chicago," Ingrid said quickly. "Phyllis called Val at home on Saturday and asked for Corrine's number. Val had to call me to get it. It wasn't until Monday that she told me what Phyllis wanted it for."

I was no longer even slightly remorseful for having "deserted" Phyllis in Chicago. I was boiling mad.

"I suppose she offered Corrine just a little more money than I'm making?" I asked.

"Oh, heavens yes!" Ingrid laughed as though I'd said something terribly clever.

It had always bothered me that Corrine had made nearly three times what I was getting, even after the raise. Not only that, but she always flew first class and never was shuffled off to a cheap hotel.

"Corrine is making twice as much as she ever made with Phyllis," Ingrid said. "And besides that, of course, Disney pays all her medical and dental insurance, and she has retirement and profit sharing, and . . ." Ingrid's voice trailed off as she looked at me. "But I shouldn't be telling you this."

I slammed into the kitchen to see if we had any wine. We didn't.

"I'm going to the store," I snarled as I grabbed my purse. I decided to walk—it would give me time to cool off. By the time I reached the market, tears were pouring down my cheeks. I'd worked so damned hard, put up with all of Warde's shenanigans, always been prompt, never letting my own considerations come before the job—I'd even missed my grandmother's funeral because we had a trip to St. Louis that week. I never quibbled about the low salary, and I'd even *thanked* Mr. B for the paltry raise he'd grudgingly squeezed out of "Miss Diller."

Well, loyalty is a two-way street and this is where I get off.

I splurged on an expensive bottle of pinot noir and trudged back up the hill to the apartment. When I got back, I found a note from Ingrid. "Having dinner with Dennis. Bruce called and wants you to call him back."

I didn't want to talk to Bruce or anyone else. I just wanted to be alone to stare out the window at the rain. Unfortunately, it wasn't raining. It wasn't even cloudy. *Hell!* I thought as I ripped the cork from the bottle. The phone rang and I let it ring. I wasn't going to talk to anyone right then. Instead, I filled my wineglass, put my sweater back on, and went out to sit by the pool. The April evening was almost balmy. Far from the cold, biting wind of Pheasant Run and a good foil for my dark thoughts.

I finally came to the only logical conclusion. I would have to quit. I didn't make enough money to begin with, and certainly not to put up with this. I didn't know what I'd do, but I knew there were plenty of good jobs out there and I would get one. The idea of a regular office job made me cringe, but I was fed up with "stars."

By the time I had emptied the glass, I began to feel better. I'd give Phyllis two weeks' notice as soon as she got home, then I'd take a few weeks off to just sit around before I'd start looking.

31

I was eager to talk to Phyllis when they returned and was fortunate to catch her in the kitchen when no one else was around. I wasted no time in telling her that I was leaving. She showed no surprise, although she offered the appropriate regret at the news. Perhaps she realized that it was inevitable. After all, I'd been with her longer than anyone since Corrine—over a year-and-a-half—and that was a pretty good run as a personal secretary to a star.

"There is something I'd like to know," she asked. "Why? Is it the travel? Is it Warde?"

Standing face-to-face with her, I didn't have the guts to tell her how I really felt. "A little bit of both. I got tired of being on the road all the time. I can't plan my social life, and while I'm forever making friends all over the country, it's frustrating to know that I'll probably never see them again."

Phyllis didn't press me further and I didn't elaborate. I didn't think it was necessary to tell her that I knew about the phone call to Corrine. What good would it do? Besides, I think she knew. She was not a stupid woman.

"Do you know anyone that might like the job?" Phyllis asked after a moment. I flirted with telling her I wouldn't wish it on my worst enemy, but since I'd made the decision to leave, I'd cooled off.

"I can't think of anyone offhand," I said. "But if I hear of anyone, I'll let you know."

"When do you plan to leave?"

"Well, I'd like to give two weeks' notice, but if you want, I'll wait until you get someone else."

"Will you stay and train your replacement?"

"Well, sure, I guess so. But I hope you'll find someone pretty soon. I've already made vacation plans for July." It wasn't strictly the truth, but I figured I had better give a definite time limit.

So it was done, and with a light heart I went upstairs to the office to tell Maria.

32

It took nearly a month for Phyllis to find a new secretary, and in that time we had several brief trips. We went to Saginaw, Michigan. A horrible experience. A group of Shriners were out in the hall partying and calling back and forth. Finally, at midnight, I called down to the front desk.

"Can you please ask these people to quiet down?" I begged. We'd traveled all day and the limo driver who picked us up at the airport regaled us with the history of Saginaw all the way to the hotel. Then he almost drove off with Phyllis's all-important wig box. It was black and blended with the trunk's interior. Had I not been watching, it would've been gone. We checked into the hotel about 8:00 P.M. and learned that there were no restaurants open nearby and the hotel didn't have room service. Warde actually made himself useful by going out to a KFC and bringing back something for us to eat.

"I'm sorry about the noise, ma'am. I'll send someone up," the desk clerk told me.

I don't know who came up or what he said, but almost immediately the noise increased and someone began marching up and down the hall banging on a bass drum.

My mother never liked Shriners. She thought they were arrogant and self-centered do-gooders, and that night confirmed it.

Sleep-deprived and bleary-eyed, Phyllis and I went to the venue the next afternoon. Talk about a small-town event—the opening act was a high-school girl wearing a red, white, and blue sequined costume while twirling a baton to *God Bless America*.

Phyllis looked at me with an expression as close to defeat as I'd ever seen. "How am I supposed to follow that?" she muttered as she prepared to dash onstage and tell them her dress was really a lampshade from a whorehouse.

From there we went to Bloomington, Minnesota, then on to Elwood, Indiana, for the Glass Festival. I was certainly seeing small-town America, and I loved it. Everywhere we went, people were kind and thoughtful. Phyllis was her usual gracious self, and I'm sure her appearance was the highlight of the year for many.

We flew on to Seattle, where she performed with the Seattle Symphony, and returned to L.A. the next day. I was really getting sick of airplanes. Finally, Phyllis told me the good news: Alexandra, the new secretary, would be joining us in Reno.

Phyllis had a two-week engagement at Harrah's, which wasn't as elegant as Harrah's in Lake Tahoe, but at least I would be staying in the hotel. I rejoiced over the basket of fruit in my room, and someone had thoughtfully given me a room at the other end of the hallway from Phyllis and Warde. It gave me a modicum of privacy.

Phyllis's opening act was John Rowles, a personable young singer. One night between shows, he told us he'd written his hit song, *Cheryl Mauna Marie*, for his sister.

"Your sister," I echoed. "But it's such a romantic song."

"It is," he agreed, "but it's also a very romantic name."

While at Harrah's, Phyllis urged me to order dinner in the dressing room so I could sign her name to the check and not have to pay for it. It made the $10 per diem a little more livable.

In a way, it was the best possible introduction to road travel for Alexandra. Phyllis had two shows every night, and she didn't have to do interviews, so it was a very laid-back gig. Besides, Reno is a beautiful little city in the mountains. Alexandra flew to Reno at the beginning of our second week. I met her in the Harrah's chocolate-brown Rolls Royce, which the chauffeur had driven right onto the tarmac. Her reaction was understandable.

"Wow!"

"Don't get used to it," I told her. "It'll probably never happen again." Then I introduced myself.

"Please call me Sandy," she said as we settled into the car. "Alexandra's my real name, but everyone calls me Sandy."

"I think you'd better stick with Alexandra. Phyllis likes classy names. I think that's partly why she hired me, because I have a hyphenated name."

She nodded and said, "When I interviewed with Phyllis in L.A., she told me that if I went by the name of Sandy Beach, every time she introduced me to someone they'd do a ten-minute riff on my name. She told me that Alexandra would be much better."

"When did you interview?" I'd known nothing about this.

"Three weeks ago. I met Phyllis, and Warde, too, at their house."

Why do I feel blindsided? This is what I want, isn't it?

I filled her in as best I could on our twenty-minute ride to the hotel. Sandy's room was next to mine, and as soon as we checked in I took her directly there so she could catch her breath before we went down to the dressing room. It was still about an hour before showtime, but Phyllis had gone down early.

Sandy opened her suitcase and hung up her clothes. "When am I going to see Miss Diller?" she asked as she finished putting things in drawers.

I called Phyllis in her dressing room. "Bring Alexandra down," she said.

"I'll show you the back way," I said as I opened an unobtrusive door in the side of the casino. We climbed down some metal stairs and emerged backstage, just steps from the dressing room. Phyllis advanced on us with tissues hanging from her nose. I felt myself get slightly sick. *What if Sandy decides this woman is crazy and catches the next plane back to L.A.?* I wondered how many more weeks it would be before another replacement could be found.

"Hello, Alexandra," Phyllis lisped as she stuck out her hand. "Welcome to Reno."

Because of her deviated septum, Phyllis sometimes stuffed tissues up her nostrils. In addition, she now wore a retainer—the final stage of having her teeth straightened—which she removed only when she went onstage. When she spoke, it made her lisp and she sounded slightly drunk.

"You remember my husband," Phyllis added. Sandy shook hands with Phyllis, then Warde.

He leered at her. "I'm pleased to see you again." I could feel Sandy tense up. "Did you have a nice flight?" he continued

"Yes. Thank you." She extracted her hand from his grip.

Phyllis intervened. "I'm glad you're here and hope you're going to enjoy the job. Now, why don't you two girls go get something to eat, and then I'll see you back here before the show."

"I'm looking forward to working for you, Miss Diller," Sandy said.

As we stepped into the hall, she said, "My God, what a couple!"

She'd been nervous, but she'd stood her ground, and Phyllis apparently liked her.

"So how did you hear about the job?" I asked as we headed for the coffee shop.

"It was sort of through the grapevine," she said. "I moved here from Chicago two years ago and have been working at a literary agency in L.A. You know, it was one of those things where somebody told somebody who told somebody else. I don't even know who found out about it in the first place. I don't know why she chose me."

Probably because you were the only one willing to work for such a pitiful paycheck. I hadn't thought I'd said it out loud, so was startled when Sandy said, "I took a cut in pay. I was really hesitant about that. Warde told me there was ten dollars per diem when we traveled, though."

"And that was the deciding factor?"

"Oh, yeah. That and a smile might buy a peanut butter and jelly sandwich at the Fairmont." Well, obviously Sandy had done some traveling. I relaxed a bit.

As we settled into a booth in the coffee shop, she asked, "So, what's Miss Diller like?"

"Don't keep calling her Miss Diller. Her name is Phyllis. If you start out calling her Miss Diller, she's going to get used to it. You can call Warde Mr. Donovan, though."

We chatted as we devoured our meal.

Sandy glanced at her watch. "About time to go back, do you think?"

I quickly realized that Sandy was organized and decisive. *She'll be perfect.* I smiled to myself. I had promised Phyllis to stay on for Sandy's first two weeks, and I could see daylight ahead—daylight and freedom!

Between shows that evening, John Rowles poked his head into the dressing room. Before long, he and Sandy were laughing together; she was starting to relax. Everything was going to work out. I could tell.

The rest of the week went by quickly, and soon we were on the private jet once again, heading for Los Angeles. We had two days at home before we took off for Houston, where Phyllis would perform with the Houston Symphony.

I was especially excited about Houston because my brother, John, lived there and we'd have a chance to visit. He joined me for breakfast early in the morning and came to the concert that night. I brought him backstage afterward to meet Phyllis and Warde. What a nice bonus for me on my last trip to get to see my brother!

This was the first introduction, too, that Sandy would have to regular air travel with Phyllis and the hassle of the carry-on bags, arrangements with limousines, the anxiety of convincing Warde to get moving on time, and all the other intricacies of traveling with Phyllis. Sandy quickly learned all that occurred with an orchestra rehearsal, and the actual performance.

On the last day, when we flew home to L.A., I kept in the background. I watched Sandy as she and Phyllis did the final packing. Sandy called down for the bellman and the limo and then did a final, quick sweep for anything left behind. As the door to the suite closed behind us, I automatically reached for the typewriter and briefcase, but Sandy picked them up and walked on ahead with Phyllis and Warde.

At the airport, the passenger service representative took Phyllis and Warde to the plane on a little golf cart. I stood quietly as Sandy talked to the skycap, took the baggage tags, and tipped him.

The flight home was uneventful. The limo was there to meet Phyllis and Warde, and they were gone before Sandy and I got out to the curb with the bags. We rode in the "baggage wagon" and chatted about inconsequential things. She seemed happy with how well everything had gone and felt that she and Phyllis had established a rapport. She even liked Warde, and he kidded with her. I tried to ignore the slight pang of—what?—*could it be envy?*

At the house, the driver carried the bags inside while I took my suitcase to my car. When I went back inside, no one was around. I heard laughter from the back of the house. I stood for a moment looking for someone to say good-bye to and felt a little awkward, even a little shy, as if maybe I didn't belong there. Then I realized, no, I didn't belong there anymore. Life had already moved on. Suddenly tears welled in my eyes as I looked around, inhaling one more time that peculiar scent of the house with its bit of sea air, Phyllis's perfume, and, gee, even a hint of dust from those same silk roses.

After another minute, I quietly opened the door and slipped out. At the end of the driveway, I turned one more time, taking it all in. Nothing seemed to have changed since the first time I saw it nearly two years before.

"Good-bye, Phyllis," I whispered. "Thank you. It was a blast."

Epilogue

Working for Phyllis Diller had a profound effect on my life. Mainly, because I married that Riviera stage manager, Bob Smith. No, really, that was his name. I moved to Las Vegas and even though the marriage didn't last, my love affair with Las Vegas has continued, and several decades later, I'm still here. Phyllis was delighted to hear that she had been the catalyst for our romance.

When going through my Phyllis memorabilia—and discovering to my dismay that I have very little—I came across a recipe with a note from Sandy, which was dated only a couple of weeks after I'd left. The note reads: "Dear Robin, Miss Diller asked me to send the enclosed recipes to you. She's decided that, as long as you are now a lady of leisure, you can be our official test kitchen. Let us know how they come out." Attached were two recipes for eggplant. I have no recollection of having made these or reporting my results back to Phyllis, and Sandy doesn't remember either. Eggplant has never been a favorite of mine—no matter what you do with the darn stuff, it is a lot of work for very little return.

However, the letter made me laugh. Phyllis and I kept in touch over the years. Whenever she was mentioned in the Las Vegas paper, I would send her the article. She'd reply with sweet little notes. We always exchanged Christmas cards.

In 2002, Alexandra (Sandy to the rest of us) threw a party to celebrate Phyllis's 85th birthday. She invited me, Ingrid, Karen, and Carole Eschler, and, of course, Phyllis.

Phyllis was in the midst of a traumatic year. Her daughter, Stephanie, had died suddenly, and Phyllis retired from show business that same month. I don't think the two were related; Phyllis had planned her retirement well in advance. Phyllis said she wanted to go out on top—you've heard the show-business admonition, "Leave them laughing." That's what she wanted to do, and exactly what she did.

So on that summer day in July, we all wondered if Phyllis would come to Sandy's party, but she did indeed. Phyllis was always one to "accentuate the positive."

Somebody else was there, too. Gregg Barson, a friend of Phyllis's, was making a documentary of Phyllis's life called *Good Night, We Love You.* Sandy had agreed he could stop by and film some of the party. Gregg and his photographer completely took over, silencing some of us in order to catch the reminiscences of others, or banishing someone else to another room so she wouldn't ruin the shot.

They stayed two hours as we sat chatting primly and laughing politely. As soon as they left, Sandy mixed up margaritas and brought out the martinis, and the stories spilled out. Phyllis absolutely howled at some of the things she heard, learning for the first time of many of our misadventures. We told of limousine mix-ups, horny stagehands, and suitcases gone astray. Warde came in for his share of bashing, but by then he was fair game. Phyllis had divorced him, finally, in 1975.

At Sandy's party I reconnected with Ingrid and Karen. Ingrid and I had remained roommates for a while until I moved to a place of my own. She and I had kept in touch, and I'm happy to say that Karen and I did as well, but I hadn't seen them for years. I met Carol Eschler, Sandy's replacement, for the first time that day at Sandy's party.

I learned some almost incredible things—Karen had not known how to drive a car when she came to work for Phyllis. A friend taught her to drive a Volkswagen. Well, no wonder she hated driving the Rolls! Carol had flown to Washington, D.C., on a presidential jet.

"Air Force One?" I asked.

"No, the president wasn't with us, so I guess not. But Sammy Davis was on it and a bunch of other celebrities. They were all entertaining at the White House."

It was fun to learn of everyone's adventures. Ingrid had gone on cruises, Sandy had gone to Australia, but I . . . I . . . had gone to London!

We had so much fun that Phyllis decided to make it an annual tradition until—literally—the day she died. Our last reunion was scheduled for Sunday, August 19, 2012. Perry sent an e-mail a few days before saying the reunion had been canceled. No explanation, but we all knew. Phyllis died the next morning, August 20. She was 95 years old.

But in the meantime, every year for those nine years following the birthday party, Phyllis invited us to her home. It felt odd to be a guest. A butler and maid greeted us, brought us champagne, and served us lunch in the big, formal dining room. In addition to the Dustbiters, as she had dubbed us, Phyllis included magician Mercer Helms, her friend and opening act for the last twenty years of her stand-up career. We were never sure if a dove would appear on the dining room table or a glass would suddenly start floating across the room. Phyllis invited other of her former secretaries to join in so that at the last reunion there were ten of us at the table.

Phyllis's very first "Dustbiter reunion" included not only Sandy, Ingrid, Karen, Carol, Mercer, and me, but someone I had not expected to see.

When I walked into the house, Ingrid came dashing up just as the maid was taking the flowers I'd brought for Phyllis. "You'll never believe who's here!"

I hesitated, feeling a tingle of fear.

"Corrine!"

Oh, lovely, Corrine the Perfect! I winced.

"Here she is," Ingrid continued, holding out a hand to each of us, and Corrine joined us.

I didn't know if Ingrid was introducing me to Corrine or the other way around. Either way, I was prepared to loathe her on sight.

Corrine smiled and held out her hand. "Oh, what a pleasure to meet you. I've heard such wonderful things about you!"

Really?

"I am so looking forward to hearing about your time with Phyllis," she said and smiled like she meant it. "Let's talk later." The butler offered me a glass of champagne.

Aw, gee, how could I be mad at this charming lady?

After lunch, we had a chance to sit and chat. The Corrine that I'd loved to hate faded away.

But years before that, before the reunions started, I had moved to Las Vegas and married Bob. He was a romantic devil and always full of surprises. They say "opposites attract" and that surely was the case. He was a night person, and I was a day person. He loved sunsets and starry skies. I preferred sunrises and bright days. He was a spur-of-the-moment, "Let's do it!" guy, and I wanted to deliberate and consider. He loved to take the Jeep off-roading and delighted in getting covered in mud. I wanted to dress up and go to the ballet. We did have one thing in common—golf. I took lessons—the ones I'd never taken

On the Road With Phyllis Diller

back at the Playboy Club-Hotel in Lake Geneva—and we played together a lot. However, we finally, sadly, realized that it was not enough to maintain a marriage. After the divorce, I got a job, bought a house, and put down my own roots.

Whenever Phyllis came to town, she invited me to her show. When she did *Hollywood Squares* at the Riviera, I took the day off to be there. (Bob had retired by then.) Oddly, Ingrid, the one who declared at the outset that working for Phyllis was only a temporary job until she got her big break into show business, was still working for Phyllis twenty years later. Eventually Ingrid married and moved to Palmdale, where she started her own public relations firm, Chapman Communications, Inc., which became wildly successful.

Because I am a Christian and wanted to make sure I would be seeing Phyllis in heaven, I talked to her about faith in Jesus Christ and salvation. I quoted the Bible's most famous verse, John 3:16. ("For God so loved the world that He gave his one and only son, that whosoever believes in Him shall not perish, but have eternal life.")

She listened politely, but truly her bible was the book *The Magic of Believing* by Claude Bristol. Phyllis's faith lay in herself. She believed that through the subconscious, and powers of suggestion and self-belief, she could overcome everyday obstacles and achieve personal happiness and professional success. Phyllis assured me that she was acquainted with God.

I sent her a book, *The Case for Christ* by Lee Strobel. She thanked me with a sweet note, saying, "Robin, darling—Don't worry about me. I have lived in heaven all my life. I know God. Love, Phyllis."

With that, I would have to be content.

At one of the reunions, I asked if I could perform a "cat rap" (see page 272). I explained that I wrote little poems for and about the cats that had lived with me over the years. Phyllis loved the poems, and every year after that asked me right away if I had a new cat rap for her. In 2010, she decided I would be her poet laureate and write her Christmas card. She had started it with "'Twas the week after Christmas and all through the house, nothing would fit me, not even a blouse . . ."

She liked the verse I wrote and painted a picture to illustrate it. She sent me a handful of the Christmas cards to send to my friends. She also sent me a hundred-dollar bill. The following April, she sent me a cartoon that had tickled her funny bone and said she wanted to use it on her Christmas card, and would I please write the verse to go with it. I did, and again she loved it and sent me a check for $100 and a handful of the cards for me to send out as well.

When Phyllis had come to the Suncoast Hotel in Las Vegas for her last week as a stand-up comedienne, I called to see if there were tickets. There weren't. I called Mercer the magician, and he promised to see what he could do.

The evening before her closing night, he called. "I got you tickets. Can you be here in two hours?"

"You betcha," I said. I took a couple of friends, and we saw Phyllis at her best.

Even though I'd heard the jokes many times and could've recited them with her, she still made me laugh. Vintage Phyllis. Afterward, she invited us up to her suite, and there was Gregg Barson still filming the documentary. He did a snippet with Phyllis and me that later appeared in the film.

The last time I saw Phyllis was in 2011 in Chicago. Ingrid e-mailed me one Friday evening in October saying, "You might get a call from the *Rosie O'Donnell Show*. They're doing a tribute to Phyllis and want some of the Dustbiters on the program." Someone from the show called me on Monday to say the show would be taping on Thursday. Would I like to be there?

Would I ever!

I'd hoped to be able to fly out with Ingrid, Corrine, and Carole Beams, one of Phyllis's last secretaries. The show had chosen four of us and arranged for our flights. The three of them flew out of L.A. I took a direct flight from Las Vegas. Because our appearance was to be a surprise, the Dustbiters stayed at a different hotel than Phyllis. She first saw us when we trotted onstage during the live show. Rosie had asked her why she had named us "Dustbiters."

"They stood it for as long as they could, then they bit the dust!" she said while making a hand motion of someone falling down.

After the show, we were invited to a dinner hosted by Richard Duchossois. Phyllis did a little intro and kept referring to Richard's "pretty horsies."

I nudged Ingrid. "What horsies?"

"He owns racehorses. Arlington Park," she said.

"Oh."

"Churchill Downs."

"OH!"

There were thirteen of us at dinner, including Mr. Duchossois and his wife. Phyllis introduced each of the Dustbiters seated at the long table. She told about Corrine being her first secretary, Carole Beams' film production company, and Ingrid's public relations firm. She told about my background in the Foreign Service, and that I had served in American Embassies in South Africa and London. Over forty years later and she remembered. Phyllis may have been ninety-four years old, but she never missed a beat.

On the show, Rosie asked Phyllis how many secretaries she'd gone through. "Oh, about forty," Phyllis said.

Forty secretaries, I thought, as I looked around the dinner table. Out of forty, I was one of the favored ones, a "Diller Dustbiter."

That was the last time I saw Phyllis, and that's the way I remember her—vibrant and happy, surrounded by people who adored her.

Memories

Phyllis Diller and Robin Skone-Palmer, 1981.

Phyllis Diller promotional postcard, circa 1970.

PHYLLIS DILLER SCHEDULE

1971 – 1972

Revised 6/1/71

May 31–June 14	(Monday–Monday)	MAN TRAP Airdate in New York WABC – Channel 7 – 9-9:30 A.M.
June 2	(Wednesday)	FASHION SHOW Beverly-Wilshire Hotel Beverly Hills, Calif.
June 3–10	(Thursday–Thursday)	DES O'CONNOR SHOW London, ENGLAND
June 16	(Wednesday)	IT'S YOUR BET Taping San Diego, Calif.
June 21–26	(Monday–Saturday)	MUSIC CIRCUS Sacramento, Calif.
June 24	(Thursday)	THIS IS YOUR LIFE – (Re-Run) ABC-TV – New York
July 12	(Monday)	HOST TONIGHT SHOW New York, N. Y.
July 12–26	(Monday–Monday)	MAN TRAP Airdate in Los Angeles KCOP – Channel 13- 10-10:30 PM
July 13–25 (19 off)	(Tuesday–Sunday)	PLAYBOY CLUB Lake Geneva, Wisc.
July 27	(Tuesday)	SONNY AND CHER SHOW Taping Los Angeles, Calif.
July 28–August 11	(Wednesday–Wednesday)	RIVIERA HOTEL Las Vegas, Nevada

A sampling of the grueling schedule of the much-in-demand comedienne, 1971–1972.

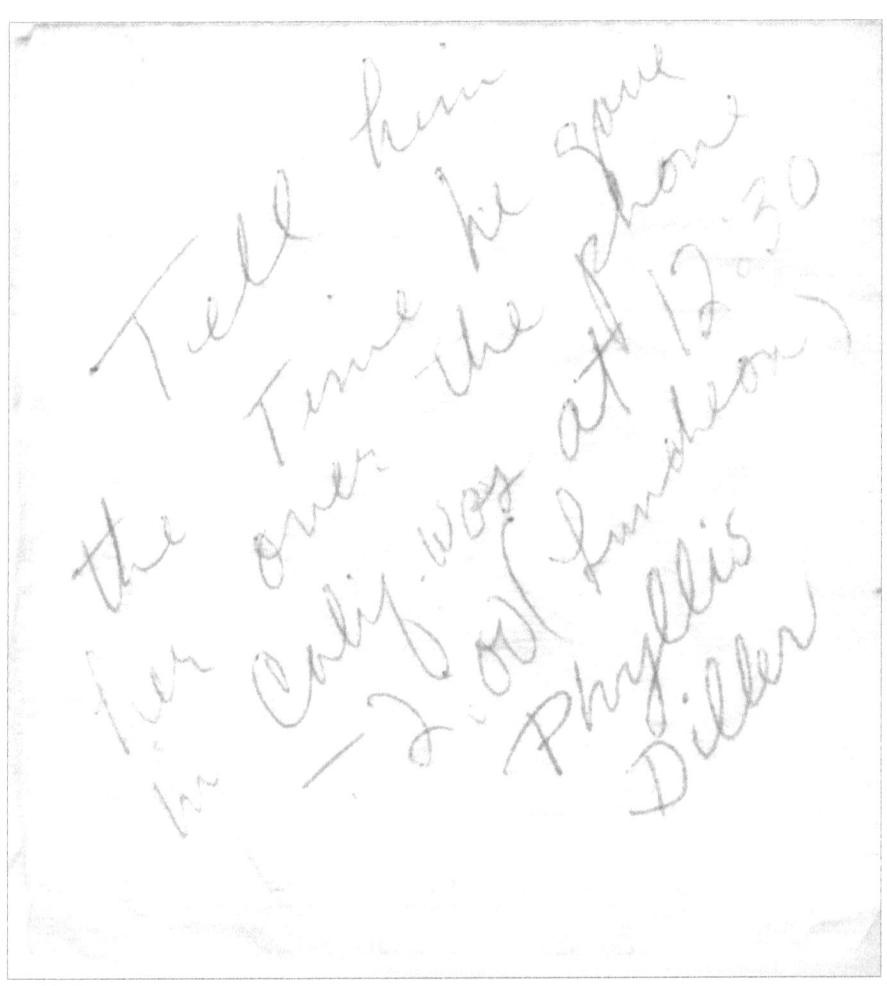

Insiders were quite familiar with Diller's propensity for jotting notes on whatever was handy—in this case, a napkin, while aboard an airplane, sent from first class to Robin Skone-Palmer in coach.

On the Road With Phyllis Diller

Diller's response after the author sent her the *The Case for Christ* by Lee Strobel.

The Dustbiters pose with Phyllis Diller in front of her painting, titled "The Spotlight," at their 2009 reunion in Phyllis's Brentwood home. L-R: Ingrid Chapman, Robin Skone-Palmer, Alexandra (a.k.a Sandy) Beach, Carole Beams, Karen China, Mercer Helms, and Corrine Hanley.

The Dustbiters were invited as surprise guests when Phyllis Diller appeared on *The Rosie Show* in 2011. L-R: Corrine Hanley, Carole Beams, Ingrid Chapman, Robin Skone-Palmer, and Karla Thomas.

Photo: Garret Boyajian

The final reunion of the Diller Dustbiters at Phyllis's home in August 2011. L-R: Jenny Cooney, Sandy Beach, Carole Beams, Heidi Rotbart, Robin Skone-Palmer, Corrine Hanley (directly behind Phyllis), Mercer Helms, Ingrid Chapman, Karen China, and Carol Eschler.

Phyllis set the date of the next reunion for August 19, 2012, but two weeks before the annual luncheon, her son Perry sent a note that his mother was not well. She died on August 20, at age 95.

Phyllis Diller beside her "Spotlight" painting, 2009.

Robin Skone-Palmer with Phyllis Diller, August 2011.

An original Phyllis Diller painting to illustrate the verse she'd asked Robin to write for her 2010 Christmas card.

'Twas a week after Christmas
And all through the house
Nothing would fit me
Not even a blouse.
I searched through my closet
For something to wear
But my clothes had all shrunk
It just isn't fair.
I didn't indulge
Well -- maybe a little
A few pieces of fudge
A bit of nut brittle.
But it's not my fault
It's the Holiday Season
I can't say "NO"
Without a good reason.
So hope you'll excuse
The rather sad fact
I'm writing this greeting
Wearing only my hat.

LOVE

Phyllis Diller

The poem inside the card was written by Robin Skone-Palmer. She and Diller collaborated on several such projects.

> Dear Robin
>   This cartoon is very pretty in color. Time to start working on 2011 XMAS card — call me so we can have high level talks
>   LOVE
>   Phyllis
>
> Your work was such a hit.

Robin's poem in 2010 was "such a hit," Phyllis asked her to write another for 2011 (right) that accompanied a cartoon of a cat in a police lineup.

I watch you get dressed to go out every night;
The glitter and glitz catches the light;
the silk and the satin shimmer and shine
Don't you think some of that should be mine?

But no one says, "Miss Kitty, would you like some nice bling?"
It wouldn't take much — just some little thing.
Those emerald clips would look good with my fur
And a lovely silk scarf would rev up my purr.

So now at Christmas you drag in a tree
And set it in the main room for all to see.
Then you cover it with jewels and all those shiny lights
And people say "What a pretty sight!"

But now everyone's looking at me simply because
I took matters into my own four paws
I mean, can't you see jewels look better on me
Than they ever did on that dumb old tree?

And my owner is saying, "Just look at that,
I'm first on my block to have my own Christmas cat!"
I'm having fun and I hope you are too,
So Merry Meow Christmas to each one of you.

LOVE

Phyllis Diller

A typical Phyllis Diller note, this one signed as "Madam," poking fun at former husband Warde Donovan, who addressed her as "Madam" when in the presence of staff members.

> Dear adorable Skone-Palmer,
>
> Thank you for your sweet note & the great photos. Stay well & happy.
>
> LOVE
>
> The Queen
> (you know)

Another thank you note to the author from Phyllis Diller, who with this signature is poking fun at herself.

THE BLACKJACK CAT RAP

I'm a little black cat, but I should've been blond. Of tuna and catnip I'm exceedingly fond.
They call me a klutz 'cause I fell off the bed. Well, I just rolled over and landed on my head.
And sometimes in the house when I'm chasing my ball, I forget to stop running till I crash into the wall.
It might be true that I really am not the absolute smartest cat on the block,
But I've big yellow eyes and silky soft fur, and if you'll pet me, I've got a dynamite purr!
The race isn't always to the swift, or the battle to the strong . . . Well, unless you're a lion.
Hey! Lions are blond!
So if you want a terrific little cat, you really can't go wrong with a little black cat who *could've* been blond!"

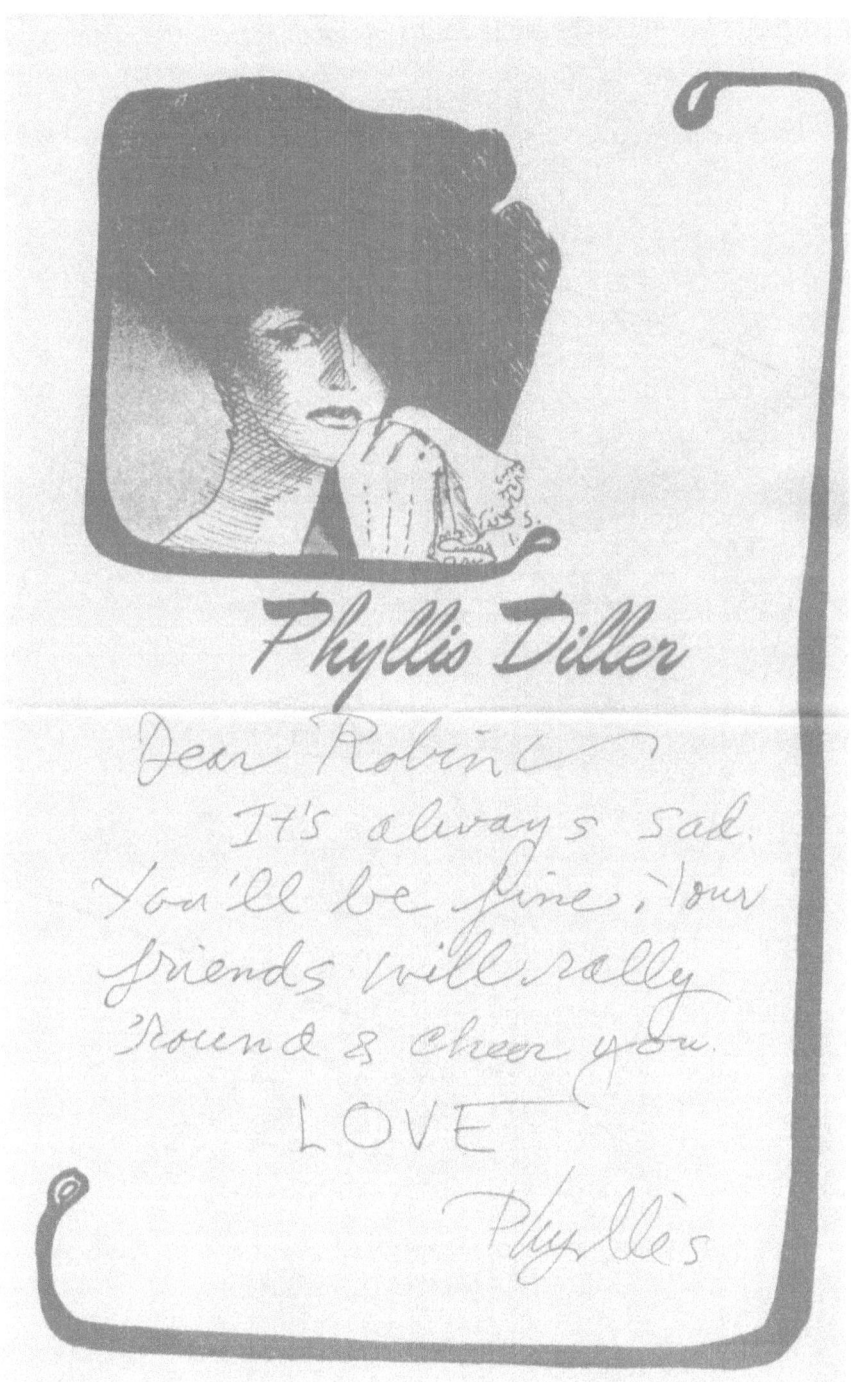

A note of condolence after the author's brother died in 2008.

A swell BOOK!
Godspeed
PD

ACKNOWLEDGMENTS

Many friends urged me to write about my experiences with Phyllis, and I appreciate their faith in me. I particularly want to thank Suzy Berg of Houston and Paula Roseberry here in Las Vegas, who continually encouraged and supported me, and never stopped asking, "How's the book coming?"

I also want to thank Lois Cadwallader for being my cheerleader. She introduced me to Larry Edwards, my editor *par excellence*, who took what I'd written and smoothed it out.

Perry Diller kindly provided the pictures of his mother for me to use, which I greatly appreciate.

Ingrid Chapman, my former roommate and avid photographer, was invaluable in providing the pictures for this book. Although she is busy running her own business, whenever I asked, Ingrid would take the time to shuffle through reunion photos to send me "the one of the Dustbiters in front of the spotlight" or "the one where I was wearing a flowered dress."

Thanks also to Mercer Helms, that wonderful magician, who sent me pictures that he took at our last reunion in 2011.

And, of course, the Dustbiters I knew and worked with: Ingrid, Sandy Beach, and Karen China, and the ones I subsequently met: Carol Eschler, Corrine Hanley, Jenny Cooney, Carole Beams, and Heidi Rotbart. I hope this brings back fond memories of your time with Phyllis and makes you smile.

For my friends and Phyllis's many admirers, I hope this answers your question: "What was Phyllis Diller really like?"

ABOUT THE AUTHOR

Robin Skone-Palmer served as Phyllis Diller's personal secretary during the early 1970s as the comedienne achieved the fame and adoration she retained the rest of her career. Robin and Phyllis remained life-long friends.

Robin also wrote poems that Phyllis used for her holiday greeting cards.

As a "Dustbiter"—a term coined by Phyllis in reference to her favorite former employees—Robin attended several Dustbiter reunions hosted by Phyllis prior to the comedienne's death in 2012.

Robin lives in Las Vegas with her two cats. She divides her time between golf, pottery, and teaching after-school Bible clubs. She also collects wine—at least long enough to chill it before she pulls the cork.

www.ingramcontent.com/pod-product-compliance
Lightning Source LLC
Chambersburg PA
CBHW031237290426
44109CB00012B/331